In a time when the world des| leadership, Rob Murray makes a compelling case to corporate leaders that getting to know and express feelings is key to their success. He offers a wide range of valuable tools for doing so and many examples, including from his own life, of the importance of these practices, which often seem counterintuitive in today's hard-edged, competitive corporate environment.

RICHARD SCHWARTZ, Ph.D. Developer of Internal Family Systems and Adjunct Faculty at Harvard Medical School

For all the "doers" and "fixers" in the world, Rob Murray challenges you to lead with heart. Rob offers a solid framework to guide your steps and brings it together with his clever, funny, and transparent personal journey. He is the real deal. How he shows up in this book is exactly how he shows up in life.

DANNA SZWED, CHRO, Ashley Furniture

There has been much discussion of late as to the need for a "new normal." While this discussion tends to orient toward proposed macro-level policy changes, Rob Murray's insightful and timely book reorients us toward the equally important micro-level emotional capabilities we must build in order to create more sustainable futures, organizations, and lives.

MATTHEW GRIMES, Professor of Entrepreneurship & Sustainable Futures, Cambridge Judge Business School

Fighting for Heart by Dr. Rob Murray is one of the most thought-provoking books on feelings and emotions that I've ever read. I offer my highest recommendation to people who want to grow in their understanding and recognition of emotions and feelings to live a more fulfilling life. *Fighting for Heart* helps refocus and recover any distortion or confusion we may have in matters of the heart.

DREW MADDUX, Executive Vice President of People Development, DSG

Rob Murray has written a book that is a must-read for any leader who either knows 'something is missing,' or who works hard at keeping up the pace of being a 'human doing.' This book is packed with research, anecdotes, and sound principles that help leaders get on track or deepen the heart-led leadership they are already practicing. I have worked with leaders for over thirty years, and I wish Rob had written this book when I started, both for me and those with whom I work. Now that he has offered it to the world, I will make this book required reading for every leader I work with.

PHIL HERNDON, Psychologist and MA, LPC-MHSP, NCC

Rob Murray is a gifted leader in the territory of emotional intelligence as it relates to leadership in the workplace. What many write about or talk about, Rob authentically lives in both his personal and corporate life. I have seen this firsthand from the front row of his life and have benefited personally by watching as many others get more of what they are looking for with his help.

JEFF SCHULTE, M.Div., Th.M., MA, LCP-MHSP, Founder & President, Tinman.life and Tinman.co

Rob Murray so powerfully teaches us that the language of the heart is the key to finding meaning in our work and in our lives. This book will help us love and lead from the heart—so we have more meaningful human connections and influence on the lives of others.

TOMMY SPAULDING, *New York Times* bestselling author of *The Gift of Influence* and *The Heart-Led Leader*

Rob's ability to take the nebulous world of our emotions and ground it in solid science, structure, and frameworks create a warm invitation into the depths of what it means to live out the human experience. If you're looking for a trusted guide to walk you into a more emotionally intelligent way of leading and relating to others, this is your book.

MARY HYATT, Holistic Life & Business Mindset Coach

Too many leaders hide from their hearts, and the consequences are material, at home and work. The work of Rob and his team has changed and challenged me to live and lead wholeheartedly. The fight is worth it. You'll be glad you read this book.

DAN CLARK, CEO, Westfall Gold

As a practitioner of Rob Murray's work over the last five years, I have been impressed by his ability to create resources, tools, and pathways for leaders to connect their heads to their hearts. The Heart-Engaged EQ System will guide you back to the life all of us were meant to lead & live. I am excited to have this work get into the hands of so many.

BRAD STINSON, Founder and CEO, Collective Global

Dr. Rob is one of the most gifted leaders I've ever had the privilege of working with. He has given light to my past and present through his thoughtful and brilliant frameworks that just make sense. His personal style is authentic while maintaining incredible depth. *Fighting for Heart* is a must-read for anyone who wants to live a more meaningful life.

BEN ZOBRIST, MLB All-star, World Series MVP

Fighting for Heart is required reading for any leader who seeks to create a high-performing team without leaving their emotions at the office door. Dr. Rob Murray has managed to balance his academic research with real-world experience and vulnerable personal story-telling to create a read that is at once credible, moving, and entertaining. It resonates deeply, and his lexicon of emotions provides a welcome and long-overdue alternative to traditional leadership offerings.

SHANNON LEFFLER, Executive Vice President of Human Resources, Geodis

In *Fighting for Heart*, Rob weaves together timeless truths with insight from his own journey in a way that makes it difficult to put down! This is the book I wish I had read at the beginning of my career and should be required for anyone who aspires to be a remarkable leader.

TONY JULIANELLE, CEO Atlas Real Estate

FIGHTING FOR HEART

DR. ROB MURRAY

WITH JEROME DALEY

FIGHTING FOR HEART

How emotional intelligence can transform the way you live, love, and lead

Telocity Media Transformative Leadership Resources Nashville, TN.

Editor's Note: The stories in this book have been used with permission, though names and identifying details may have been changed to protect the privacy of those mentioned in this publication.

ISBN 978-1-7359352-2-5

To my wife Natalie, your compassion and kindness have changed me. Thank you for your tireless support and championing throughout my messy, clumsy research and practice of feelings.

To my beautiful children Noah, Ella, Viola, and Adia, I will offer you my recovering heart with a promise to fight for yours all the days I have breath in this life and the next. I really like, love, and adore each of you.

To Jeff Shulte, I am forever grateful for your painfully earned experience that guided me through my past to start recovering my heart. You awakened me to a deeper awareness of myself and those I love and serve.

To Jack Nicholson, Your care, belief, and investment in my life has been both humbling and rare. You have modeled and embodied the true nature of a Sage. You have helped me honor the survivor and welcome the builder.

Lastly, to all the leaders who have courageously showed up to fight for their hearts in my groups, cohorts, and retreats . . . you have pushed, challenged, and motivated me to keep showing up!

TABLE OF CONTENTS

FOREWORD

I WAS OUT FOR A JOG THE OTHER DAY, trying to get this big-boy body in shape. As I stopped at an intersection, waiting for the cars to pass, a white 4Runner pulled up beside me. Inside the vehicle was a mother and three girls, whom I guessed to be in their early to mid-teens. Intrigued, I watched as the mother talked animatedly to the girls, all three of whom had their heads buried in their cell phones, disengaged and uninterested in anything she had to say.

The scene saddened and unsettled me.

As I thought more about what I witnessed, I recognized that the kids and their cell phones were not the biggest issues here. The responsibility for leading and transforming families should primarily fall on the shoulders of engaged parents.

What also troubled me about the situation was how it paralleled the relational dynamics that can play out in organizations daily, mine included. And like the parents of these girls, I should be held responsible, along with my team, to invest in the systems, structures, and actions that can cultivate and support the growth of healthy leaders and culture in our organization.

As the CEO of Dufresne Spencer Group (DSG), dba Ashley Furniture HomeStore, I spent an exhausting amount of time trying to create the most transformational culture in all of retail. I desperately wanted our core values, "Love, Home, Team, Trust, Winning," and our vision, "Life-Moments Matter," to permeate everything we did. It's not all about the furniture; the lives of our employees and coworkers matter most. These values and vision extend to our customers as well. We are learning to sell customers a vision for a home rather than a piece of furniture for a house.

But no matter how much information, motivation, intelligence, or data I poured into our people about living a better life and their homes mattering more than the workplace, I failed to see the level of change I set out to achieve.

I recall sitting in a meeting with my executive team, asking them what percentage, from zero to one hundred, they believed we had transformed our culture over the past fifteen years.

The highest score I received was 50 percent, and the lowest was 10 percent, with the norm coming in around 25 percent. *Something is wrong. Something is very wrong*, I recall thinking. Ultimately, I had adults across my company who were struggling to establish trust because of the massive fears inside that kept them from effectively communicating and connecting in ways that matter and drive healthy companies. I realized that many of these leaders would look at me and, without actually verbalizing it, say something like, *I don't really know if my contributions truly matter here, and despite working hard, I never quite know whether I'm enough.*

I realized I could try to be everybody's friend or set the table and create a platform for those in our organization in ways that would affirm my friendship and, more importantly, support their lives and leadership.

After realizing this, I invited Rob Murray and Jack Nicholson from Transformed Leader to help me better understand what I needed to do to engage my heart and the hearts of my people. How could I help change people in a way that would help them live boldly, creating a future they believed they were worthy of and that they had what it took to succeed? Rob's work gave me the language and keys to demystify the heart of leadership, and his leadership frameworks unlocked the door to transforming our corporate culture all across the country.

Our mission was clear. With Rob's help, we would transform the culture one leader at a time because, as he says (supported by the research and the numbers), "the heart is worth fighting for." Our DSG team began to work with Transformed Leader to create a transformational ecosystem to systemically engage our leaders across the entire organization. Part of that game plan led us to create Legacy Life Groups, each made up of ten to twelve leaders, to go through a three-month developmental experience designed to recover the heart and soul of their leadership in ways that they could reintegrate into their home and work lives. As the company's CEO, I was a little apprehensive about whether the employees would lean into this work. I had all types of executives in the room, from vice presidents and directors to managers, but wow, they not only leaned in but dove in.

One thing I love most about our investment with Rob has been the sessions on emotional intelligence, which is what this book is about. I didn't realize how essential feelings were to leadership, and I also didn't know how much more there was to emotional intelligence than feelings. It's not something that we talk about. In fact, any talk of feelings in a business or leadership setting is generally discouraged and frowned upon. Most businesses see feelings as a sign of weakness. We could not have been more wrong.

There are several voices out there at the intersection of emotional intelligence and leadership development. Still, very few offer a practical pathway or roadmap like Rob does through his system, books, and consulting. He does a masterful job of helping leaders learn how to identify, name, and communicate what is happening inside them, so they have more to work with on the outside. When there is alignment and congruency in a person's internal and external realities, the sky is the limit.

The book you hold in your hands is more than nice words and good ideas. These concepts come from the blood, sweat, and tears of leaders fighting for more of their hearts in the marketplace. I have seen my leaders dive deep into this material, and it changed them.

When leaders ignore their emotional system, they grow numb and miss out on new opportunities for growth and wholeness. That's not the energy and spirit of transformative leadership.

You'll see a shift in people in the first session who say, "I can't feel," to seeing those very same people standing up and articulating their feelings with clarity in the last session. You'll hear and see the embodiment of freedom as they realize what it's like to be human again. I'm watching this sweep through my organization like a West Texas wind, and it's changing the hearts, lives, and leadership of my people.

Frankly, I've seen Rob and his team accomplish more in the hearts of my people in twelve months than I was able to achieve in fifteen years. It is art, research, and science, and it is beautiful to see. I'm watching it transform my culture across the country. It is the most fun, rewarding, and fulfilling work I've done as a leader since beginning my career.

Don't get me wrong. We always did a great job of executing and getting results. We had a ton of data, intelligence, and information, all above-the-line items. I had created a world-class organization, but we had not yet reached our full potential. We were not living and working from the heart.

Today, we are leading out of who we are. It's not all about what we're doing; it's about both who we are and what we do. Working with Rob and his EQ system has transformed our lives, our corporate culture, and our interactions with our customers in profound ways.

I'm confident this book will do the same for you.

Chad Spencer
CEO at Dufresne Spencer Group, LLC
dba Ashley Furniture HomeStore

DR. ROB MURRAY

 **HAILING FROM** Cape Town, South Africa, Rob moved to the United States in 2002 and over the last twenty years, he has worked at the intersection of Leadership, Business, Faith, and Social Justice. This journey led him to complete a master's degree in social & civic entrepreneurship, and a doctorate of transformational leadership.

As a co-founder and CEO of *Transformed Leader*, Rob fosters a deep passion for developing transformative resources and approaches that systemically help coaches, leaders, and teams engage deep-change strategies, both personally and professionally for themselves and those they serve. Franklin, Tennessee, is home (for now) to Rob and his wife Natalie, and their four beautiful kiddos.

www.drrobmurray.com
www.transformedleader.com

INTRODUCTION

Before I can tell my life what I
want to do with it, I must listen
to my life telling me who I am.

PARKER PALMER

"STEVE, YOU LOOK EXHAUSTED. And it sounds like you have been for a long time. How much longer do you think you can hold out before this all hits the fan?"

I sat across the desk from the senior vice president of sales at a large telecom firm. The desperation in his eyes was unsettling. But familiar. I had seen it so many times before. Steve's organization professed to be human-centered, progressive in its HR policies—vested in a holistic workplace environment for healthy teams. The reality was, ah, somewhat different. In truth, it felt more like a convenient fiction from top to bottom, a glossy cover to entice new candidates into the machine.

"Who knows, Rob," he responded with a sigh. "I can't see a way out. Every day feels like a referendum on my loyalty. The only way I can prove I'm a team player is by being on call 24/7. I'm expected to answer emails within minutes and be continuously available on apps, chats, phones, meets, video, office drop-ins, and every other communication channel-of-the-month. If I'm not on tap at every moment day or night, I'm met with passive-aggressive remarks, thinly veiled threats against my yearly bonus, or some snarky comment that hints at my unreliability. I sleep five or six hours a night. Exercise has gone by the wayside. I'm taking meds for stress. I love what I do, but this place is starting to feel more like a prison than a workplace, and the CEO is clearly the warden. They're not bad people, but this is becoming a bad place. Bad for me at least."

Listening to Steve's story, I felt my own emotions well up: sadness, grief, and anger at the fore. Internally, I acknowledged their presence but asked them to hold the tension for now. It would do Steve no good at this point for me to check out on his feelings by voicing my own. There might be a time for that, but for now, it was enough to offer him space to express and unravel his emotions. He seemed relieved to unburden himself. Clearly, he was carrying a crushing load—one that threatened to wreck his life, here and at home.

He continued, "I'm trying to hold it all together at work only to walk in at home at night and feel like a stranger in my own house. My wife has worked hard to find a job after losing the last one, but it's not working. I think she's given up, and that means the pressure has doubled down on me for our survival. I try to love her and support her as best I can, but I'll be honest: I feel trapped on a sinking ship. She's already under water, and I'm close behind."

The oxygen felt thin in his spacious, well-appointed office, and we both paused to breathe. Trophies of Steve's academic and corporate achievements adorned the walls while also taunting his distress.

"I hear you, Steve, and I want you to know I see you as a brave leader, fighting long and hard for your family and for an organization that may not exactly see you for you but rather for what you do. To survive, you've numbed out, trying to tamp down on emotions that feel dangerous. It's the human thing to do, but it only works for so long. Eventually, your suffocating heart will break down that door and show itself or be locked away so deep and far away that you may never find it again. That emergence can be channeled in positive directions, or it can burn down the house. I'm here to help you figure out how this story is going to play out."

You could see the war between hope and hopelessness in his eyes. He was really tired. I watched him struggle to discern whether he could risk allowing his heart to beat again. It had become hard to unsee what I had reflected back about the state of his union. The silence lingered until he finally took a deep breath, looked me in the eye, and said, "Okay. Let's get started."

An Invitation to Recover Your Heart

I work with leaders like Steve every day, across a vast spectrum of industries. Many are hearing some version of that same message: "Get up, get out there, and deliver results. You can't stop, and don't you dare drop. It's not enough; *you're* not enough. Go faster, bigger, better. Prove yourself."

Wait a minute. *What's the point of all this fear and drivenness?* Who even knows anymore? The leaders we talk to are paying a high price, both in relationships and productivity at home and work, in environments that fail to foster emotional connection and growth. Something essential inside us is dying. We are losing some fundamental element of the human experience.

Maybe you carry some aspect of Steve's story in your story: exhaustion, isolation, loss of meaning, and identity. Does anyone have solutions for these honest needs? I believe there are genuine answers and that it begins with letting our emotions out of the closet in a safe, skilled environment.

In this book, I want to offer you an invitation. I'd like to help you recover your heart and be able to use your heart powerfully and unapologetically in every aspect of your life, including the business arena. I want to give you practical ways to infuse your leadership with self-awareness and human connection. I think this book will be different from others you may have read: I focus first on how to be *Formed*, so that you can then better *Perform*. The language of the heart is the key to finding meaning in our work and the fuel for thriving over the long run.

We know the opposite of Heart-Engaged leadership all too well. This pathology embedded in modern life and leadership centers around losing our core. Our heart. The emotional center of many of us has become so impoverished that we lead out of emotional bankruptcy. Even when we are connected in mind, we are often disengaged in heart. The connective tissue of relational health atrophies, and deep inside, we know something is dreadfully wrong. Teamwork has become utilitarian; collegialism is a thin veneer for desperate networking and posturing. Nobody can long survive the absence of heart without paying a tremendous price.[1] Isn't it time we change this story?

Fighting for Heart offers leaders, teams, and organizations a roadmap for strengthening your internal core. From an engaged core, you will better manage and appreciate your own emotions as well as those with whom you live and work. It's like moving from monochrome to color; life simply becomes more alive. More vibrant. More compelling. In short, it opens the door to the things that matter most.

As you begin the journey to become a Heart-Engaged leader, it will not only change you personally; it will transform your influence on those around you. I want to give you the tools to transform anxious-driven organizations. Instead of being sympathetic, you can become empathetic. Instead of being reactive, you can become responsive. Instead of being considerate, you can become compassionate. Instead of conclusive, more curious. Heart-Engaged is heart-smart.

Fighting for Heart will deepen your emotional growth and leadership effectiveness, as many counseling centers, therapists, leadership coaches, consultants, and companies are already discovering in their work with the Heart-Engaged EQ System. Whether you are interested for the sake of your organization or simply for your own life and relationships, you will find an approachable and accessible path in these pages for living and leading with more heart.

My Awakening

If you've read my first book, *The Human Operating System*, then you know some of my own story of awakening. I was thirty-six years old when my wife walked into the room one day and asked if we could talk.

Uh-oh. This can't be good, I thought, but I faked calm and answered, "Sure."

Sitting down on the edge of the bed, Natalie looked at me earnestly. "Rob, you're a great dad to our four kids and a good husband to me. You're working so hard to take care of us—building your business, finishing your master's degree. You provide well, you love us, you're totally committed to us."

I nodded cautiously, hearing a "but" coming.

"But . . . I miss you. I want more of you. I'm lonely. So often you're here physically, but you're not really here. Do you think there could be another way for us to do life that would include me getting my husband back?"

A hundred protests died on my lips as the weight of her words crashed in on me. In a moment of absolute clarity, I knew there was real truth here. With Natalie's support, a good guide, and a lot of personal work, I was able to rediscover and re-engage my heart in ways that revitalized my soul, my marriage, and my business leadership. It was one of the most important decisions of my life, and I hope it will catalyze a similar transformation in you.

Like many of us, I learned to reject, numb, and hide my heart at a young age. As a result, I grew into an adult with no idea how to recognize or access my emotions in any productive way. Feelings in my family were more often avoided and managed than invited, expressed, and processed. So I never learned how to find healing for the inevitable wounds of life except by being more defensive, independent, or self-sufficient. And I became really good at these things.

Thankfully—and tragically—the world of commerce welcomed me into an environment where these impairments could be leveraged for success. An old-fashioned family wound can be an incredible motivator for driving leaders to work harder, faster, and longer than anyone else around them. I embraced that opportunity to a degree and gained some tangible benefits, but that path couldn't take me where I most wanted to go, especially as I was starting to enter the second half of my life.

In the most vulnerable and unedited of moments, my heart would bubble up uninvited. Nagging questions would emerge and preoccupy me: *Who are you, really? Do people really want you? Behind all work and activity, what is it you really want? And are you enough to get there?*

I was tired of feeling alone . . . and feeling afraid . . . and of not even being able to name the emotions I felt. I was tired of trying to suppress the voices so I could get back to work and keep trying to prove myself. The invitations of productivity, entertainment, and success could no longer stifle my heart's desire for intimacy and connection. I wanted to be productive, but I also wanted to know others deeply and be known in return.

At this point, we simply can't afford to keep moving forward without one of our greatest assets: our feelings. We have to slow down long enough to catch up with ourselves, to reintegrate, and to try this thing a different way—the way we were meant to live—*wholeheartedly.* Have you grown accustomed to leading with your feelings on life-support, then trying to resuscitate them just before you walk through the door at the end of the day to greet your family? Then maybe we can agree that it's not working anymore. Maybe it never really was. We can survive such dissociation for a while, but eventually, our hearts rebel. Either that or our hearts simply fade away and start to wither.

As a society, we stand on a precipice together: a new era of self-discovery and meaning we have longed for all our lives. Social prophets across all fields are saying as much. Just a few decades ago, people were shamed for investing time and energy on themselves, or worse, being in therapy; now we have research professors like Brené Brown and Susan David charting a new way forward within a mainstream audience. It can be both interesting and inspiring to read about how to be a better you, how to incorporate spirituality, or how to breathe more deeply. These are great personal topics, but now we're learning that these things matter even in the staid world of corporate management and entrepreneurship. If it's true in one place, it's true in every place.

The corporate landscape is desperate for a less mercenary, less competitive, less toxic atmosphere, and we can only get there if we start paying attention to our hearts. Just as we have learned to pioneer new technologies, financial tools, and economies of scale, so we must turn our attention to something more primal. More fundamental to our humanity. Does this speak to something true in you?

It's no secret that the most expensive line item on just about any corporate budget is payroll. People. Losing and replacing people is enormously expensive. So even if companies can't quite bring themselves to invest altruistically in a healthy culture, they need to understand this priority from a purely financial interest. It's a smart business decision to help teams integrate their hearts into the workplace mix; it will save them money. And as a bonus, it will help people make better decisions, synergize their gifts, and actually want to go to work in the morning.

I think it's time to call a ceasefire on the civil war

between our insides and our outsides, and this happens when we learn to accept and process our feelings in skillful ways. When this takes place, everyone wins: the leader, the family, the community, the organization, and the culture at large.

Think physical fitness for a moment: You may have great intentions to work out and even buy a gym membership, but at some point, you will need to get in your car, drive to the gym, and lift those weights if you want to add muscle. This book offers a conceptual framework and then a tangible plan to guide you toward practicing your feelings as well as recognizing and respecting those of others. You'll still have to do the work, of course, but I'll make it easier by providing a roadmap and a compass.

In this book, I want to help you see more of yourself—parts that have been squelched or silenced. I want to help reawaken your connection with the people and things that matter most in this world. I'll open this book by building a case for the values and benefits of an emotionally resilient leader. This work is personal, but it is also backed by research that validates the positive impact on healthy leaders and organizations that push through emotional stagnation into bold new levels of growth.

I'm determined not to leave you bloated on inspiration and ideas. Instead, I'll give you a practical, effective pathway to guide your steps in deepening your emotional life and leadership. I'll say it now and it bears repeating: *You can't grow EQ solely with IQ.*

I would make for a bad emotional poker player. My most obvious *tell* is the word "whatever." My wife knows that when that particular word rolls off my tongue, it is usually a reaction to my most vulnerable feelings. "Whatever" is the declaration of my protective walls going up—the need to avoid facing some level of hurt, rejection, or pain.

This word, informed by my brain's survival intelligence, gives me permission to step away from anything and anyone that feels like a threat. Unfortunately, this coping mechanism often undermines the growth opportunity embedded in the situation: learning how to express my feelings and then finding a courageous response.

The tools and perspectives we will explore in this book are the result of my having to learn these truths the hard way. Despite the time it's taken me to integrate them into my life, they have strengthened my leadership like little else, and I believe they will do the same for you.

Here is a preview of where we're headed: *First*, we're going to learn how to check in with our full humanity and notice where our bodies, minds, souls, and hearts are located at the moment. *Second*, we're going to learn how to identify our feelings and listen to their feedback. *Third*, we're going to explore the internal "characters" and figure out how one or more can guide us forward. And *fourth*, we're going to reach intentionally for the outcomes we most need in our professional and personal lives.

If you're tired of chronic inertia in your effectiveness and a vague haze over your closest relationships, welcome aboard.

No longer do you have to shut down the core of your humanity. No longer do you need to bluff your way through the complexities and vulnerabilities of life. If you can't lead from the truest part of yourself, why bother? It's time to recover our hearts together and bring our whole selves into the richness of this beautiful world. Are you ready?

CHAPTER 1

HOW DO YOU FEEL ABOUT FEELINGS?

*When we can talk about
our feelings, they become
less overwhelming, less
upsetting, and less scary.*

MR. ROGERS

FRANK CAME TO ONE OF MY WORKSHOPS last year and, as trust and vulnerability emerged during our work together, began to unburden himself in the group. (Please note that this story, along with all the others in this book, has been adapted and incorporated with the permission of those involved.)

"My wife and I will be married ten years this fall, and I can say that over the past five, I have lived in a state of near-constant fear. Fear of my words, fear of my actions, fear of my emotions, my addictions, and my pain. I'm not sure who's to blame for these struggles, and I'm not even sure that's the right question. But the reality is that I'm in a marriage in which I feel the need to watch my every move from a defensive, reactive posture. It's exhausting, and I don't know how to change it."

The rest of the group sat in rapt attention with concern and empathy etched on their faces. A few nodded as if their own journey may have mirrored Frank's.

"It's less about the marriage itself," Frank continued, "and more about what intimate relationships do to me. I've come to realize that I live in a pervasive anxiety *that I'm not enough.* That I may never be enough. And that one day, she's going to figure out I'm not enough *for her* . . . and leave me."

"Thank you for sharing" is a standard response in the types of EQ groups we facilitate. We don't try to take away the pain; instead, we try to offer space and create a compassionate witness that can help leaders feel their feelings and listen for whatever wisdom the feeling may have to offer before picking themselves up to do something about it. "Are you willing to say more about your fear?" I prompted.

"This may sound strange, but I'm not sure if I'm actually *experiencing* fear. I'm afraid of fear, so I hold it at arm's length. I try to subdue it, to lock it down so it doesn't wreck me. When it peeks out, I try to muscle up and just get through whatever it is. I go to my faith, go to my self-help book collection, and even to some of my friends. I get a quick shot of adrenaline, and things feel better. For a month or two. Then my deeper beliefs about myself start to creep back in, and the fear begins to stalk me again."

The more Frank talked, the more animated he became. Apparently, it was cathartic for him to bare his soul in a safe place. He knew we wouldn't try to "fix" him with cheap advice or projected solutions. Instead, our goal was simple: to listen and help people explore their hearts with courage. We can't exile our troublesome parts just because they are troublesome. We have to let them say their piece and determine whether their message is helpful or not before we can right-size their voice and recalibrate it in light of our whole self.

Frank went on to describe how anxiety and self-doubt have bled into nearly every part of his life. And that's the thing about feelings; they don't usually stay compartmentalized. They travel. And the more we try to squelch them, the more we wind up strengthening them.

"The tragedy is that those closest to me know about it and yet have no idea what I need. And of course, neither do I. I'm just trying to pull on the thread of this experience and see where it leads me."

In that setting, we gave Frank permission to explore. We listened. We cared. We were present to the constellation of feelings he acknowledged. And as he talked, the pressure seemed to ease. By the end of the group, his troubled countenance had visibly relaxed and was replaced by clarity, peace, and perspective. Frank still had work to do, but now he knew he wasn't alone. And no longer did his fear of not being enough need to tyrannize his thoughts or marriage without his knowledge. His feelings weren't the whole truth, but they were genuine voices of truth. In time, his emotional awareness would help him press into new levels of growth and trust.

Curiosity and Courage

Our values and beliefs on most topics have been shaped by the marinade of our personal stories and cultural backgrounds. I was born and raised in South Africa where the culture is pervasively expressive and engaging, much like the whole of Africa in general. Someone familiar may reach over to hold your hand while talking to you. This is a physical expression and symbol of that person's attention, closeness, and connection to you personally within the noisy crowd. It is a physical way to say, *I see you and I'm with you.* You could walk up to a group of construction laborers and start singing a familiar song, only to have them drop their tools and enthusiastically join in. That's Africa.

I am grateful for the emotional expression that has textured and deepened my British lineage. Yet these cultural norms have not entirely translated into my westernized experience in the United States. Here, I would be quite nervous to grab someone's hand in a noisy convention center to affirm he or she has my attention. I would need a good attorney on speed dial. And breaking out into song in public . . . not so much. I'm pretty sure I would generate confusion and concern.

The West has largely privatized the internal life. We build expansive back decks and avoid our front porches. We connect only if it's convenient and scheduled. We pull into the driveway, hit a button to open the garage door, and enter directly into our houses without any exposure to neighbors. The very nature of our architecture has reinforced the message of our internal detachment. Is it any wonder that we have a loneliness epidemic on our hands?[2]

We humans are a complicated species, full of complexity and tensions. What you say may not reflect what you believe; what you do may not reflect how you feel. As you journey with me, I hope that curiosity and courage will be your guide. *Curiosity* will crack your heart open to new possibilities that fall outside your current assumptions and practices. While we spend much of our lives trying to survive emotions, the cultivation of curiosity can be an incredible practice to draw us into the land of the living.

Courage is the other necessary ingredient for your journey. Without courage, it is nearly impossible to venture beyond the comfort and safety of our fortified existence and defenses. Courage invites us to face and process our fears in ways that produce brave action. If you're not at least a little afraid about something, you won't need much courage to lean in. I hope you actually have a small amount of trepidation by the theme and messages in this book. The leaders we work with are hungry for a challenge; they want adventure. I have found the eighteen-inch journey from head to heart to be one of the bravest adventures I've yet undertaken. Curiosity will call you to try new things while courage will necessarily fuel the engagement.

The Formation of a Mindset

I have spent significant time in my life and career researching, studying, practicing, and being mentored in the field of emotional intelligence and resilience. Specifically, my doctoral dissertation led me to study the intersection of emotional intelligence and leadership development. As part of my qualitative research on the topic, I explored the effects of the emotional preferences of the family of origin and how those effects yielded a dominant emotional mindset for a current generation of leaders. The results are sobering.

Describing the emotional influence of the mother, 50 percent of respondents stated that emotions were expressed but in an aggressive, frightening, unpredictable, or weaponized manner. One that destabilized the family system rather than nurtured it. And 40 percent reported their mothers taught them to avoid or suppress their emotions in the home. Only 10 percent affirmed that the mother's influence cultivated the safe expression of emotion.

The emotional influence of the father was equally concerning: 70 percent reported fathers who were avoidant, suppressive, and governing; 30 percent reported that the way in which their fathers expressed emotions left them feeling scared, which leaves 0 percent reporting a healthy emotional context from fathers. It's enough to make us wonder how anyone survives growing up. Even when we know on some level that we *are* loved, the actual experience of *being loved* at a heart level is hard to access.[3]

The outworking of these family-of-origin stories will surprise no one. Among the participants in my research project, almost everyone identified emotionally avoidant as their operative condition and only one participant identified unhealthy-expressive as their default. None of my participants claimed to emerge from their family of origin with a healthy model for emotional expression. And of course, these are the nascent dysfunctions we inevitably bring into our own marriages and parenting until we learn new ways of being in the world.

Can we learn new ways? Can we build new mindsets with new tools? Absolutely. But will we? Will you?

Your Emotional Lens

Entrenched across the depths of our communities, companies, and cultures at large are varying perspectives and beliefs around the validity of emotions. *Are feelings good or bad? Do they help us or hurt us?* As a result, I have become keenly aware that these simple questions are answered in predictable ways that yield three predominant positions on the subject, with a rare fourth (a healthy version of the third). Identifying with one or more of these responses will offer some fresh perspective on how you were raised emotionally and the journey that has brought you to the present day. This simple act can be a powerful first step toward becoming a Heart-Engaged leader.

It's important as you read the upcoming sections that you practice what I suggested in the previous section—stay open and curious about your life and story. Try being exploratory, not conclusive. You will recognize and relate to parts and pieces of each of these three stances, and that's good. As you read the different stories that accompany them, try to relate;

you may uncover echoes of your own past. The rules and emotional posture of various members in your family of origin may appear.

You may also notice similar or different dynamics in your current life. Maybe you retain the beliefs you had about feelings since you were young, or maybe these beliefs have shifted and evolved over time. For some, the predictable competitiveness of transactional commerce has been a welcome respite to replace volatile family systems. Others may find themselves shocked by how the ruthlessness of the marketplace contrasts with the value and appreciation they experienced growing up.

Catalyzing a movement to shift the corporate landscape feels daunting, but as Gandhi encouraged, *we can ourselves become the change we hope to see in the world.* The leadership benefits of clarified emotional mindsets will set us apart. The things we do and say, the ways we treat others and ourselves are heavily informed by our relationship to feelings, and we may not yet be aware of it. The benefits of emotional intelligence will shape the foundations of our own lives, and in time, our teams, organizations, and communities. Changing the world begins with changing ourselves.

Posture #1: Feelings Are Bad, Avoid Them

Feelings are dangerous. Feelings are unpredictable and threaten us with loss of control. Feelings skew reality, and the only antidote is to ruthlessly repress them lest we be swept away in chaos. This was James's subconscious default, and we're going to hear his story next. Strong leaders, James believed, rise to the top through restraining the corrosive influence of emotion with iron-willed determination. This worldview may lie unnamed and unspoken, but its influence is pervasive, informing most behaviors and decisions being made by leaders, teams, and organizations.

By the time James was eleven years old, his disruptive childhood led him to believe that feelings were wrong, or at the least, unhelpful. In their formative years, James and his siblings did not experience safe connections or consistent love. As a result, they did not form healthy attachments with their parents. Provision yes, nurturing no. His parents were young and overwhelmed by circumstance, doing the best they could with what lay in arm's reach. Their tumultuous relationship finally came to an end, splitting parents and siblings down the middle.

Confused by a plethora of unnamed inner currents and with no one and nowhere to express them, James wondered what was wrong with him. Why did he feel so tender and needy? Why couldn't the hurt and fear go away? Why was he so desperately searching for safety and security from those who seemed absent and unavailable? Life was simply undecipherable, and the only way to survive was to shut down those aspects of the heart that now felt like a threat. This is the story of many who come from homes where feelings were mismanaged or avoided altogether.

As a young adult, James learned quickly that feelings were

not his friend. They were scary, unpredictable, and shameful. Feelings were not helpful in any practical sense, except for a few "good" ones. His feelings only served to trigger reactions in others, and that didn't work to his benefit very often. Since no one seemed to have a handle on them, the obvious solution was to stuff them down. Way down. Out of sight and out of mind.

The unaccounted cost of this decision, however, was that James began to believe he was flawed. Overly sensitive. Too vulnerable. He had to thicken up his skin, armor up, accept his lot, and get on with life. In unedited moments, though, the repressed sadness, hurt, and loneliness would well up, and he would scramble to distract himself with entertainment or adrenaline. The last thing the world needs, he intuited, is another lonely, ungrateful soul.

But loneliness is not so easily thwarted, only masked. And as James entered adult relationships, he found intimacy elusive. The workplace, even, became a place where he could achieve but never belong. The cost of emotional safety, it seemed, was emotional isolation.

Adapting and Coping

In the face of such distress, we want to give our parents an "out"—*They did the best they could*. And while it may be true, sometimes, a person's best simply isn't good enough. The consequences of parents' limitations and brokenness bleed down the line to those they love the most: their children.

I am learning to accept, voice, and process the humbling realities that my own intentions and actions as a parent, spouse, friend, and leader will often fall short. I have resolved that I will get it right maybe half the time, but if I can show up to the other half when I fail, I may offer those around me the opportunity to grow from the experience rather than be buried by it.

Many of us learn, indirectly or directly, to associate feelings with moral judgments against ourselves and others. When healthy expressions of emotion are not permitted in a family system, children are forced to learn how to express, reach, and need in other ways. When there is no safe place for them to express themselves, they learn to repress, rage, or medicate.

And so, James abandoned these placeless parts of his humanity to focus on more useful ones—like coping skills. He learned how his charm, intellect, and internal drive could propel him forward to perform well on the outside and earn shades of the approval he so desperately craved on the inside. As Pia Mellody, a nationally recognized expert on emotional dysfunction might say, his "adapted teen" replaced the "wounded child" and set the stage for the "functioning adult."

As James ventured into early adulthood, he resolved to become needless and wantless. Bergstrom notes that when someone arrives at a conclusive sense of needlessness, they will inadvertently seek other ways to satisfy the needs that failed to be met.[4] For James, needing and wanting people only proved a continual disappointment, so he repurposed those desires toward school, performance, morality, and chasing girls. *The irony of the last two . . .*

The best and worst of childhood typically get carried over into adulthood. What you do and how you think now is informed by the collective stories of your past experiences. James discovered pragmatic ways early on to avoid his "insides." He learned to push up and out as quickly as possible when life got overwhelming. Denial, distraction, and determination are the "three Ds" of survival I have identified in my own life. Can you relate?

Children and adults alike use these resources to escape forces that feel unmanageable. In the field of recovery, we no longer shame these responses because we know that they helped us get through hard times when allies were unavailable. We find more compassion for ourselves and for others. It's important to note, however, that these strategies have a shelf-life. If deployed for too long on old traumas, they infiltrate and sabotage the possibility of new narratives and outcomes. Leaders who avoid the past often struggle to break into new areas of personal growth and development.

From a corporate perspective, you may hear things like, "Check your emotions at the door when you come to work." This paradigm highlights a dark reality: You're entitled to your feelings; *you just can't have them here.* Unless, of course, we're talking about good feelings. Practically speaking, the suppression of feelings temporarily aids organizations that care solely about the bottom line.

Mary, an executive I worked within the non-profit sector,

shares her story. "Growing up, feelings weren't allowed in my family, and they still aren't. My dad is around, but he doesn't show up much. Sharing anything beneath the surface makes my mom highly uncomfortable, and when she gets uncomfortable, she gets angry." You may relate to parents like these. Or perhaps you *are* those parents. One of Mary's parents is apathetic while the other is aggressive. Mary has had to grieve those losses and release the hope that either of her parents will pursue a meaningful relationship with her or her children. She explains:

When I try to share any level of emotional expression, I am immediately shut down and shamed for being *too much*. I realize now that this isn't going to change, and I've reluctantly agreed to the 'emotional family rules' to salvage at least some level of relationship with them. It's not what I want, but at least it's something.

I wish they could be healthy because they're the only parents I have, but the cost has gotten too high to be a real human around them. I need safer places and safer people where I can be authentically me.

Dr. Lindsay Gibson, a researcher on emotional intelligence, concurs. "[Emotionally immature people] can probably never fulfill your childhood vision of a loving parent. The only achievable goal is to act from your own true nature, not the role-self that pleases your parent. You can't win your parent over, but you can save yourself."[5]

With emotionally stunted parents or bosses, here are typical responses to emotional disclosure:

- "I don't care how you feel. Just pull yourself together and get it done."
- "Stop being so dramatic."
- "Don't let them see you sweat."
- "Get over it. Just let it go already."
- "Crying is for sissies."
- "You're too sensitive."

Four Types of Emotional Immaturity

I've mentioned apathetic and aggressive parents as examples of people with diminished emotional capacity who are threatened by the emotions of others and respond with various self-protective strategies. Gibson builds on this idea extensively in her book, *Adult Children of Emotionally Immature Parents*, describing four different types as Passive (apathetic), Rejecting (aggressive), Driven, and Emotional.

I'll start with the last first because the dynamic is counterintuitive. *Emotional* parents (or co-workers or other family members) are terrified by the emotions and needs of others because those feelings threaten their own emotional stability; their coping strategy then is to weaponize their own emotions to shut down any emotional expression. Anger and shame are the typical weapons of choice in this abusive dynamic.

Driven people appear healthier and are able to affirm others at some level but only when those others do things that meet their needs. They can tolerate your feelings as long as they experience them as *good* feelings. If you're happy, they are available to you. If you're not, then they aren't. When life gets real, you'll have to find someone else to be in it with you because they are unable or unwilling. The primary aim in life for *Driven* people is to move forward toward a goal, and feelings may be an impediment to that. Or so they believe.

Rejecting people are the most painful among those who believe that feelings are bad. They use their emotions to intimidate anyone who dares to express themself. Once again, anger and shame are the most easily accessible tools for this work of repression and domination.

Finally, *Passive* people are the least aggressive in their mission to shut down the heart, but no less damaging. When you need them, they are nowhere to be found. Your emotional needs send them scurrying off into hiding and communicate loudly, *You're not okay. You're too much. My emotional equilibrium is too fragile to deal with your issues, so stay away until you get a grip.*

While uncomfortable to admit, I can relate and identify with all four of these immaturities in some way. Gibson's categories have helped provide language and perspective for some of my behaviors when it comes to both parenting and leading.

Most of us have been affected by these people and these dynamics. And sadly, most of us have also been the bearers of some combination of passivity, rejection, emotionality, and drivenness toward others. It's only when we can flush our fear of emotional expression to the surface and learn skills for healthy expression that we can break our cycles of emotional poverty that damage one another, which is why I have written this book.

Fortunately, we now have tremendous tools at our disposal for rewriting the script of our emotional fear, and we're going to map the way. First, let's look at the next major category that describes how people feel about feelings.

Posture #2: Feelings Are Data; Analyze Them

While many believe feelings are bad and should be avoided, some believe feelings can be extremely valuable. From this posture, emotions are data points, available to be analyzed and understood. Feelings are packets of information that should be noticed, processed, and used toward achieving positive outcomes. In and of themselves, they are signposts. Socially neutral—neither good nor bad. Just tools.

Stephen is a successful marketer and a highly driven individual. Despite his good looks, strong work ethic, and financial success, he is unable to find someone to share his life with. Stephen is well into his forties and lonely. Working hard and unattached in his twenties allowed him to outwork anyone, anytime. Now, though, he is looking back over his life and wondering where it went. No children, no significant other, nobody to come home to at the end of the workday to share life with. His friends are unrelatable, and it's only getting more awkward and sad for him.

Waking up one day, Stephen realized he was desperate for change. He needed someone outside his predictable cycles to disrupt his cemented mindsets. To see the things he couldn't see about himself. A sense of urgency welled up inside his heart.

"A friend told me I need to call you," he admitted to me on the phone. "He said you move people, and I need some movement. Badly. I'm stuck." Stephen was spot on: I love inviting movement. I can't create transformation, but I know how to invite it.

"Stephen, how do you feel about feelings?" The answer to this simple question would help me understand his past, his conditioning, his mindsets, his levels of resistance, and more.

"Feelings . . . um, they're fine. Feelings are feelings. They are dopamine releases. They are right up there with a good movie, sex, a new job, and so on. Enjoy the good ones, deal with the bad ones, and move on with your life as best you can."

Not a bad answer. Understandable. But a lot of great data was going to waste in Stephen's journey toward the life he wanted. The good news was that he was further along in his emotional development than I anticipated. At least he recognized feelings as a legitimate part of life rather than avoiding them at all costs. His indifference was still hurting him, but it was a start.

Things got clearer as we talked. What emerged most strongly was a hesitancy, actually an outright terror, that his feelings would undermine his professional performance in some way. *You can have feelings, and I want feelings, but let's not allow them to rule us. They have a time and place.*

Stephen was open to harnessing his feelings to the extent that they would help him work harder and smarter, but that was all. The crux of his stuck-ness was being one person at work and trying to be another in his personal life. The capacity for empathy, tenderness, and connection remained elusive, and his loneliness was proof positive. He tried to fake it, but his own disbelief bled through and became obvious on dates. His distrust and even disgust with emotions tainted his personal relationships and desire for human connection. Something had to change. He had lost heart and was fed up with the results. Fortunately, desperation opens the doors of possibility for change.

Becoming an Emotional Scientist

Before we go any further, let's name exactly what we mean when using the term "emotional intelligence." I am partly defining it as our ability to recognize, express, regulate, explore, and integrate our feelings.[6] In a later chapter I will be expanding this to a clearer, more concise definition that I have uncovered through my research and practice. There has been tremendous expansion in this academic field over the last few decades. Insights from psychology, biology, brain science, and other fields have converged to pierce the veil of understanding on how emotions shape our lives. As we will see in the next chapter, emotions are now being explored through the lens of quantifiable variables that can be tracked, traced, and measured.

Becoming a student of my own feelings and those of others has added great value to my life. It helps me differentiate between *the data of feelings* and *the feeling of feelings*. I've discovered that when leaders start noticing, recognizing, and analyzing these emotional markers in their bodies, it helps them to make better decisions, consider alternative behaviors, and deliver more integrated results.

Marc Brackett writes, "All emotions are an important source of information about what's going on inside of us. Our multiple senses bring us news from our bodies, our minds, and the outside world, and then our brains process and analyze it to formulate our experience. We call that a feeling."[7] Brackett's contributions to the field of emotional intelligence over the past twenty-five years have changed the way we understand the role of the heart in life and leadership.

I share his advocacy, encouraging people to become a student of their own inner lives and environment. The emotional landscape of leadership is untapped and underdeveloped. Typically, leadership energy focuses on the efficiency of managerial operations. There is ample training on becoming productive but very little on integrating our emotional data toward competency within the landscape of commerce. So we have a choice. We can either wait around until the industry catches up, or we can make the transition now to emotional literacy.[8]

As bold adventurers, we have the chance to become curious and proficient in the realm of emotional intelligence, which is not as scary as it sounds. When we shrug off the aura of intimidation that surrounds matters of the heart, we will find the confidence to learn and grow as human beings. Our relationships will begin to thrive. We will connect more intuitively with those we lead while inspiring others to do the same.

Becoming a student of your feelings is only the beginning of the adventure—a vital step that brings insight, invites curiosity, and opens possibilities. But it takes one more shift in posture to actually apply that data in the real world of work and relationships. Scientific research alone can be clinical. Cold. Lifeless. When was the last time you casually read a doctoral dissertation for fun? I just finished writing one, and I can promise you "fun" is not an adjective I would apply.

The process of aggregating information can be highly instructive, but now we need to translate it into real life. I want to introduce you to a pathway that pairs becoming an emotional researcher with becoming a heart coach. When these two skillsets come together, then you're on your way to becoming Heart-Engaged.

Posture #3: Feelings Are Human; Accept Them

Through my own journey of study, experience, reflection, and personal work, I have come to believe that feelings offer us both data to analyze and also, humanity to accept. Emotions are what make us human, and I am coming to embrace the truth that, whether they feel good or bad, they are a priceless part of my human experience. As we accept this reality, we begin a healthier relationship with our feelings.

There is a tendency to choose sides in the uncivil war between logic and emotion in our lives, but we can do better than a cease-fire. In the midst of the challenging experience we call life, head and heart can be reconciled in ways that unlock the very beauty and goodness that make life meaningful. This reconciliation opens the door of opportunity for your logical and emotional centers to collaborate as peers and partners rather than contend against one another. These great allies are meant to complement and resource one another as we navigate life day by day.

There are two versions of this third mindset, however. One expression categorizes those who are emotionally accepting and expressive but may feel scary to be with. They can unpredictably fluctuate between excitement, passion, intensity, reactivity, and chaos at any given time. This is the "feel your feelings" kind of person, but they don't seem to have a handle on what is happening inside them. Emotions may be welcomed and accepted, but they don't have the structure or emotional intelligence to support their position.

The other expression of this worldview outlines the mindset I am advocating for in this book and with the Heart-Engaged EQ System. Feelings are human, accept them and do so safely and intelligently. Learn how to strengthen your heart and give voice to your inner world in a way that invites

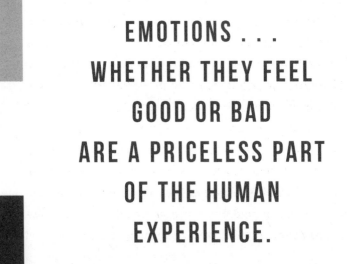

EMOTIONS . . .
WHETHER THEY FEEL
GOOD OR BAD
ARE A PRICELESS PART
OF THE HUMAN
EXPERIENCE.

and challenges others to consider doing the same. Emotions are welcomed but stewarded. Feelings are part of the human experience and attempting to dismiss them (avoid) or study them (analyze) will limit the full scope of your opportunity to experience the richness of life.

How exactly did feelings pull the short straw? We all have bad thoughts, but it's not like we say, *Thinking is bad*. We cherish our bodies and our minds, but feelings somehow became intrinsically suspect. Bad feelings can be miserable and bad thoughts can be detrimental, but we have to find a more comprehensive way to recognize and accept the benefits and liabilities of each. I call these the "gold" and "shadow," and we'll unpack them more later.

Here is a simple diagram to illustrate the primary mindsets most people ascribe to in some way. And remember, it's likely that one of these mindsets is your primary foundation, but it's also common to overlap and blend several. As you become a student of yourself, start paying attention so your mindset can be reworked and become more whole.

FEELINGS ARE BAD	FEELINGS ARE DATA	FEELINGS ARE HUMAN
AVOID	ANALYZE	ACCEPT
		⋏
		SCARY HEALTHY

Several years ago, I walked into Janina's clinical office needing someone to help me finally face a challenging relationship in my family—a relationship I had avoided for too long. I had shoved the repressed trauma and turbulent memories down deeply, but not deep enough to keep them from damaging the rest of my relationships.

I figured that the only way forward would be to go back and reprocess my story with some professional guidance, and I was willing enough. Having already stepped into the "emotional scientist" role, I had learned various frameworks on the topic by this time. It has always been easier for me to study my life than live it. To compartmentalize my feelings than to actually feel my feelings. Being the scientist is easy; you can observe from afar. But Janina was having none of that.

"Rob, you love trying to figure everything out. I can see you trying to figure me out, trying to understand my process, my methods. You desperately want to know all the facts and tools so you can be in control."

"Yes, I'm aware of that," I replied evenly.

"Well, I want to say kindly that this part of you is noisy in our sessions. It takes up a lot of space in the room. As long as that voice dominates, it's going to be hard to hear the deeper, quieter parts that also need to be expressed. How would you feel if we asked Figure-It-Out-Rob to stand down just long enough to access some other parts of you?"

"You could do that for me?" I asked incredulously. Working so hard to understand everything really is exhausting. As a kid, I honed the habit of figuring out all the moving parts as a strategy to feel safe. Reading a room, grasping concepts, anticipating information—these skills helped me experience some sense of safety in the turbulence and storms. In an ever-changing landscape of home life, I became a smart, savvy survivor. While this part of me was an asset in my past, and still sometimes in the present, it was getting in the way and hindering my growth.

Maybe you can relate to being able to talk about your story but not necessarily enter it emotionally. You may be good at presenting the data, but you're not necessarily connected to the experiences that hold those data points. That's okay. We're all in process. What we're learning here is that the freedom to know *and embrace* your feelings is essential to entering the fullness of the human experience. It is the evolved posture of an emotionally healthy leader, and that's where we're headed together.

Humanizing Your Leadership

Ernest Becker, author of the Pulitzer Prize-winning book *The Denial of Death*, shares a sobering reality throughout his message that suggests to live fully is to live with an awareness of the rumble of terror and danger that is ever-present in and around us at any given time. Accepting the realities and limitations of our existence invites us to consider proactively the resources of heart, soul, mind, and strength to usher us into a fuller life. The life we're meant for, as leaders and as humans.[9]

Feelings are built into our human design, and they offer us a window into the world, inside and outside, that comes from nowhere else. As such, they must be validated and honored as the rich resources they are. They welcome us to explore and accept what they offer rather than try to marginalize or control them. Truly, heart and soul are what set us apart from the rest of creation.

In my work through Transformed Leader, we guide leaders from a transactional experience of life into more transformative potential, and we have helped a host of individuals and teams connect to their hearts in these very ways. With life-changing results. We have watched clumsy first steps begin to restore the blood back into their bodies as eyes brighten and the inner light begins to shine once more. Our driving passion is to humanize the leadership experience, knowing that commerce and society have so often achieved the opposite effect.

I have always loved the serenity prayer that targets the contentious truth of being human. *Grant me the serenity to accept the things I cannot change, the courage to change the things I can, and the wisdom to know the difference.* Acceptance invites strength. Courageous engagement with the heart activates change. Feelings grant us the chance to connect meaningfully with our world. What begins as emotional science leads us inexorably to integration, building emotional capacity and resiliency.

It's important to acknowledge that emotion is not always used responsibly or skillfully. Our shadow side knows how to weaponize feelings like a destructive tornado, terrorizing people and leaving a path of debris in our wake. Passion without maturity is like giving car keys to a child; he or she isn't ready to handle the enormous responsibility behind the wheel. And we saw the ways emotions can be mismanaged in Gibson's model of four emotionally immature archetypes.

My vision in this book is to teach you how to drive, responsibly and joyfully, as you become a Heart-Engaged leader.

Don't Party at My Funeral

I'm sure you've heard people say how they want their funeral to be a time of celebration and laughter—a full-on party rather than bleak mourning. Something along the lines of, *Please don't be sad. This isn't a time for tears but for joy.* And while the sentiment sounds noble, it betrays a tragically Westernized truncation of feeling.

My friend Jeff would periodically teach groups how he hopes people will be gutted at his funeral: "I want my life to have meant something, enough for my family and friends to be deeply sad when I die, and for a significant amount of time. Grieving me would be the ultimate honor of my life and what I've meant to them." Those words have stuck with me.

When we avoid feelings, we have to check out or distract ourselves during times when feelings are meant to be felt. When life asks us to engage in the fullness of the human experience, let's rise to the challenge. Sure, there is an authentic way to celebrate someone's life when he or she dies, but without an equal measure of grief, the "celebration" rings hollow.

When something precious and irreplaceable is lost, the most honest human response is sorrow. When we try to divorce ourselves from the painful end of the emotional spectrum, we find that we inadvertently lose our capacity for the joyful end as well. Emotional richness comes with emotional breadth. Celebration and grief need not be irreconcilable.

The Heart-Engaged leader is one who has done the work to expand his or her range of emotional feelings and expression in order to lead with more depth of character. Without this expansiveness, life is essentially dulled and dialed down to a nub of its human potential.

Where From Here?

I have worked with leaders who have attached themselves to each of these three postures: Some believe feelings are essentially bad (except for the good ones), and we should avoid or minimize them. Others believe feelings are just data, neutral packets of internal information that should be identified, utilized, and managed appropriately. And still others have come to accept their feelings as the most human part of themselves and are learning how to accept, process, and appreciate them accordingly.

As a reader, you come into this book with your own experiences and opinions about the role of emotions. I hope that in the pages to come, we can offer some compelling reasons to move beyond the "feelings are bad" posture, to become an Emotional Scientist of your own feelings, and then begin to embrace the priceless gift of all three intelligence centers—body, mind, and heart.

The truth is, some feelings do feel bad, and it's logical to protect ourselves by avoiding them. Such defensive maneuvers make sense, given how scary the world can be at times, but building an impenetrable fortress around your heart will come at a cost. Sure, those walls reduce the likelihood of being hurt again, but they also limit your capacity for growth and relationships. It's a lonely existence.

To become the best version of ourselves, we must move beyond this posture and enlarge our emotional capacity. To legitimize feelings as useful data points. And from there, why not take it a step further and begin to accept that feelings are part of our greatness? That healthy, strong, and centered leaders will be those who engage their hearts to enlarge the character and substance of their lives.

I mentioned that avoidance comes at a cost. Do you know what else comes at a cost? Doing nothing. To ignore your own development in heart intelligence sets a hard ceiling on your capacity as a human and a leader. For the emotionally undeveloped, there are simply conversations you can't have, decisions you can't make, and groups you can't inspire. Both work and home are too important to marginalize in this way.

This is a great moment to pause, here at the end of this chapter, and do some work around your emotional mindsets. Reflect on how you were raised, conditioned, and shaped. Consider your relationship with feelings, and with curiosity, explore how that mindset has helped and hurt you. This isn't about judging yourself or others; it's about catching a glimpse of your true self, who you're meant to be. Instead of dragging an anchor, emotional dexterity can become your superpower.

Let's ditch the old ways of thinking about feelings. I'm tired of strategies that focus solely on defense, aren't you? Let's make a conscious decision together to remove stunted, reactive approaches to wellness and become proactive and skillful. This is the fork in the road facing motivated individuals and their organizations. If you want to avoid being held hostage by emotions, yours and others, it's time to fight for your heart.

How do you feel about feelings? I hope you feel differently now than when you started this chapter. Ask yourself that question frequently and listen for your heart's answer. It's time to start paying attention to these vital markers. This step alone will strengthen the bond between your cognitive and emotional systems and set you apart from the crowd. Your relationships, decisions, and overall well-being will be the beneficiaries.

Among those who have decided to answer the fight for heart and join one of our EQ groups, I found three key motivations:

- *They recognized emotional disconnection and wanted more for themselves and their core relationships.* This usually gets flushed to the surface by some kind of painful situation.
- *They wanted a safe place to connect, emote, belong, and be supported in this kind of growth.* Nothing is more

central to the human condition than the need to belong.

- *They were invited by a trusted friend, counselor, or group facilitator and said yes.* Opportunities mean nothing until we decide to accept them.[10]

In the following chapter, we're going to say yes to the next step. We're going to place this conversation about Heart-Engaged Leadership squarely within the expansive field of emotional intelligence. We also want to contextualize Heart-Work within the full range of *The Human Operating System*, my first book. And from there, we are going to build out a simple but robust pathway for harnessing your heart energy to become a fully integrated and empowered leader. Ready to fight for your heart? Then let's go.

CHAPTER 2

WHAT "THEY" SAY ABOUT FEELINGS

*The heart has its reasons which
reason knows nothing of.*

BLAISE PASCAL

GEORGE WAS A RESTLESS SKEPTIC, not unlike many leaders who wind up mandated by an employer to work with a coach. His boss had gone through a transformational experience in one of our cohorts and deeply wanted the same for his executive leaders. George felt ambushed, having no idea what he had been signed up for. Or "sentenced to," as it felt at the moment.

"Respectfully, Rob, I'm not quite sure what you guys do, but I'm not much of a toucher, a feeler, or one of these kumbaya culture warriors. I doubt I'm going to fit in with what you're doing here." He looked at me, waiting for a reaction. I listened curiously.

He continued, "My team are all high performers. Numbers are up, so I couldn't be happier. So again, no offense intended, but I feel like I'm wasting my time here. I don't know what else to tell you."

It's not the first time I've heard this. In my line of work, I'm constantly engaging with established, proven executives who have spent a long career getting stuff done, making and managing copious amounts of money for themselves and their organizations. I understood his resistance. He could confidently run circles around this young, forty-something leadership consultant (me). I appreciated his forthrightness.

My initial response in confrontational moments like this is to trust and use the same frameworks you will learn about in this book. First, I check in with myself to find my center. I start to notice what I am feeling and how my body is reacting. I touch base with my reactions, defenses, and insecurities. Finally, I reach the intersection of calculated conviction and humble courage so I can respond, not react. I remember to use this tool once in a while, and get it right fifty percent of the time. Thankfully, this was one of those moments.

I shared with George how his boss had sent him in the hope that he would stretch his leadership capacity and deepen his character. "Speaking as a thrifty South African, why don't you at least consider taking advantage of two paid days away from work. Our time will only be valuable to the degree you are willing to show up. George, I am really good at what I am really good at, and you are really good at what you are really good at. Maybe there is an opportunity here for us both to learn and grow in new areas. What do you say?"

My frankness caught him by surprise, and I saw his wheels starting to turn. I continued, "For a minute, let's forget about what your boss wants, and let me ask if there's a personal or professional leadership challenge you have right now that's keeping you up at night?"

George was unfazed. "Rob, in my line of work, there is always something keeping you up at night. But my dad used to tell me that if you get up, shut up, and get on with it, you'll be able to climb to the top of any ladder you want!"

"Wow, George, your father would have been proud to see you now. How do your wife and kids feel about how that approach has played out in your life with them?"

Silence. His jaw tightened as he held my gaze.

"Well," he answered slowly, "They are definitely grateful for the good life I've provided and all the nice things we have." I watched him soften just a bit. "But if I'm honest, I think they want something more from me. I had planned to retire last year, but when I was offered a significant promotion, I took it without telling them. They've been upset. They'll come around, though. I'm sure of it."

But George didn't look sure.

"I've been trying to get them to understand how this decision will set us all up for more."

"Set them up for more of what, George? More money, more houses, more what?"

George sighed and suddenly looked tired. He took a

minute before responding. "I'm not sure I even know anymore. My wife wanted to start traveling and invest more time with our grandbabies, but that will have to wait."

"You've certainly provided well for your family. I know that's important to you. And your boss says you're one of his highest performers. Well done. So, let's try again. What else could your family want from you?"

"Rob, I have no clue. Maybe . . . maybe they want more *of* me."

"That's very possible, George. It's certainly true for many executives. In our line of work, we help connect the *doing* and *being* parts of leaders so they are more human at both home and work. Sounds like they want more of who you *are*, not just what you *do* for them. You're a lucky man. What if we pull on the thread of this a little more?"

In a matter of minutes, I watched George connect to the parts of his humanity he had abandoned. His posture shifted, his defenses came down, and he began to open up to the moment.

"George, it's possible I'll never see you again after these next two days. What if you trusted me to help you recover some missing parts of your heart and soul so you can connect more meaningfully with your family? We can start there, and I'm pretty sure this growing wholeness will bleed into your leadership at work too."

"I'll give it a try, but don't try to make me cry. Last thing I need is becoming a softie like these Millennial snowflakes."

I laughed. "All right, George. No guarantees, but all right."

I have found that when leaders are willing to work at the edge of their growth, either personally or professionally, the other is naturally affected. For George, he couldn't initially imagine he needed to change anything on the professional front, but the work he did over the next two days indirectly, and eventually directly, transformed how he valued and inspired his team like never before.

He never overcame his father's words entirely, but he definitely became more human in his office. Emotional growth on the home front began to soften some of his intensity on the work front. Later, he told me he only wished he had learned these tools decades before. I have personally witnessed, countless times now, that leaders who grow emotionally perform better at work and help foster a healthier corporate environment. That's why I care about emotional development.

George was initially resistant to anything heart-related. His generational mindsets, along with his father's vow and the influence of a capitalistic corporate culture, had taught him that great leadership was only about being smart and working hard. The challenge for George, though, was that despite the high numbers, his team members experienced him as relentlessly pressuring and aggressively competitive (same for his wife and kids). His team not only made the highest numbers, but they also had the highest turnover. Employees had to climb or die under his leadership; there was no place for being human on his team. Yet over the next year, all that started to change.

Pushing Through the Barriers

We've been talking about the massive walls that resist any element of emotion or vulnerability in the workplace. And it's easy to understand why. From its earliest origins, America has been a "build it" culture, an action culture, so stopping to smell the roses has not been much of a priority. There are times for "doing" and times for "being," but the best leaders cultivate both, even in build-it mode. The leaders we are developing are agile in synchronizing head and heart rather than defaulting to merely one.

Considering how America has focused on growth and building during the last few hundred years, it makes sense that *doing* stuff has been an exaggerated priority in the world of commerce specifically. Here on the tail end of the industrial and mechanical revolutions, effective leadership has been defined as smart, logical, and reasonable. With enough brainpower and willpower, you can deftly climb the ranks of any organization. Sure, there's value in investing in relationship skills—to the degree that they can help you climb and build faster—but it's no secret that the business world has an unspoken pact to gate check your emotions at your office door so you can work faster and harder without the "distraction" of feelings.

Despite our advancements, I am constantly reminded how we do the things we believe are right, only to learn over time that they are not. Are you old enough to remember when smoking on airplanes was an unchallenged idea?

Apparently, Bayer Laboratories put heroin in their cough syrup until 1910 when someone finally determined it has some unusual addictive properties. Go figure. Cocaine was used not so long ago as an additive in drinks and medicines to add a little skip in your step. Swallowing tapeworms to lose weight anyone? Ah, the good old days.

All this to say, just because something becomes acceptable for a season does not necessarily mean it's good for you in the long run. I believe we have gotten it wrong by suppressing and exiling the emotional dimensions of humans in the marketplace, thinking this would help us focus on making better companies.

The results are in, and that's a fail.

Let's consider some of the great advances in various fields that invite us to recover the heart in ways that benefit all of life. I hope you realize my work in this book is not a fancy new idea. I'm not a pioneer in this space, but rather one of a host of early-ish adopters who knows this stuff makes people and the world better. I offer my ideas and processes in the context of a growing movement of researchers, educators, practitioners, and business leaders who believe that *the best companies over the next century will be those who develop wholehearted leaders and organizations.*

In this chapter, I want to offer a brief summary to highlight a few of the major contributions from the field of emotional intelligence, specifically related to the necessity of reintroducing the heart into the world of commerce. Consider this case that supports my work rather than just taking my word for it.

If you're more of a cut-to-the-chase person and want to do your own research, you can skip forward by giving this quick questionnaire to three to five people on your team:

1. Would you like me to treat you like a human or a machine?
2. Would you like me to care about what you do, who you are, or both?
3. Would you like to grow your relational capacity or lead like a sociopath?

I'm hoping your answers run "human, both, and non-sociopath," and that you have already discovered the value of heart-engagement in your own office. I hope it leaves you hungry for strategies that deepen the integration of EQ and IQ in your leadership. For the rest of you, let's skim through some highlights of the industry.

The Science of the Brain

Smart people have been studying the brain for a long time now, and we have yet to unlock the full complexities of human design. I'm grateful, however, to have access to a growing body of research that informs my leadership.

I have become fascinated with research in the field of interpersonal neurobiology and other neurosciences that overlap and relate to emotional integration, and I'll offer just a quick pass over a few voices to whet your appetite. Mark

Waldman and Chris Manning invite us into new territory with these words:

> Tucked away behind the folds of the neocortex are two of the newest evolutionary structures of the human brain: the insula and the anterior cingulate. They contain special neurons that give you profound powers of perception. They enhance your ability to be self-directed and socially aware, but remain largely underdeveloped in your brain for decades.
>
> Recent brain-imaging studies have proven that you can consciously strengthen these neurons and the connections between your social brain, your decision-making brain (your frontal lobes), and the emotional centers that shape your desires and levels of happiness.
>
> When you stimulate these complex circuits through mindfulness and self-reflection, something remarkable happens: negative feelings and thoughts are transferred into optimism, your motivation and creativity increase, your decision-making skills are enhanced, and your ability to empathize with others rapidly grows. Compassion increases, self-love soars, and a new 'voice' can be heard, one that will guide you towards greater awareness and serenity.[11]

Fascinating.

Psychologist and neuroscientist Lisa Feldman Barrett is making waves through research that overturns the more established views on emotional development. She pushes against the notion that emotions are automatic, universal, and hardwired in different brain regions. She instead makes a case for how each emotion is constructed through a unique interplay of brain, body, and culture.

"The classical view of emotion," Lisa posits, "is the idea that somewhere lurking deep inside you are the animalistic engine parts of your brain. There are circuits—one each for anger, sadness, fear, disgust and so on. And that when something happens in the world to trigger one of those circuits—say, for fear—you will have a very specific facial expression, a very specific bodily response, and that these expressions and responses have universal meaning."

That's all wrong, reports Barrett synthesizing research from neuroscience, biology, and anthropology to construct a radical new theory of emotion.

"The problem with this set of ideas is that the data don't support them. There's a lot of evidence which challenges this view from every domain of science that's ever studied it."[12] So, emotions aren't happening *to you*, Lisa contends. Your brain *makes them* as you need them. Emotions aren't reactions to the world; rather, emotions actually construct our world. We are the architect of our own experiences; it's just that most of this is happening outside of our active awareness.[13]

Developer of interpersonal neurobiology (IPNB), Professor Daniel Siegel, illuminates the practical application of these insights this way: "Consider the difference between saying 'I am sad' and 'I feel sad.' Similar as those two statements may seem, there is actually a profound difference between them. 'I am sad' is a kind of self-definition, and a very limiting one. 'I feel sad' suggests the ability to recognize and acknowledge a feeling, without being consumed by it. The focusing skills that are part of [this perspective] make it possible to see what is inside, to accept it, and in the accepting to let it go, and, finally, to transform it."[14]

The Pioneers of Emotional Science

The scientific field of any discipline is constantly evolving and shifting. My favorite people to be around are those who are in a constant state of curiosity and intrigue, despite their current knowledge on a topic. As someone has likely said, interesting people are those who are always interested. While researchers continue to probe and inform us about how emotions are made and why, let's take a quick step back in time to the origins of our inner-space exploration.

If you have ever been to a therapist or counselor's office, you have likely been asked the question, "How are you feeling?" The question is geared to bypass the logical parts of your brain and access the more experiential dynamics taking place inside you.

The *Cambridge Dictionary* defines a psychologist as, "someone who studies the human mind and human emotions and behavior, and how different situations have an effect on people." Did you catch it? Psychologists work at the intersection of mind, heart, and strength. That sounds just about right.

Many have contributed to the vast field of psychology that has so shaped our understanding of the emotional dimension, perhaps none more that these recognizable names: Sigmund Freud, Carl Jung, William James, Ivan Pavlov, and Alfred Adler. These pioneers dedicated their lives to probing the mysteries of the mind, and establishing theories both diverse and resonant. Let's take a quick tour.

Although his early work focused on the fields of biology and physiology, Freud was one of the first to be captivated by the frontier of the human mind and the observable behaviors it generated. Intrigued by French experiments using hypnotism to treat hysteria, his own exploration was inconclusive. Freud began to pursue the idea that many psychoses and phobias originated from traumatic experiences of the past, now hidden from conscious awareness. He helped clients recall these hidden experiences and confront their intellectual and emotional content, leading to healing of the neurotic symptoms.

Jung began as a student of Freud, only to become a colleague and eventually a competitor. While Freud focused on past trauma, Jung became excited about what he called the collective unconscious—the invisible connections among all things—as the necessary avenue toward *individuation*, the ability to use both the conscious and unconscious mind. The access points of dreams, myth, religion, and art helped form his personality theory that led him to describe the human psyche in three parts: ego (consciousness), personal unconscious, and collective unconscious.

William James, a brilliant psychologist and philosopher, played an instrumental role in bringing psychology to the United States and establishing Harvard University's psychology department. James framed emotion as a secondary reaction to physiological reactions, a revolutionary concept that turned contemporary beliefs on their head. And even though modern research now limits the extent and scope of this concept, James's emphasis on the role of emotions was a huge step forward in his day.

Most of us have at least heard reference to Pavlov's dogs. A biologist more than a psychologist, Ivan Pavlov nevertheless made striking discoveries in animal behaviorism that have shaped our understanding of human behaviorism. Specifically, the effects of reward and punishment upon our emotional decision triggers have defined much of the scope and strategy in modern marketing and leadership. Pavlovian conditioning now refers to a stimulus-response connection that is hardwired into our emotional biology.

Alfred Adler completes our speed-dating round with some of the most influential minds in psychology. Adler's original theory focused primarily on the human need to feel noticed and appreciated. He proposed that contentment was generated through positive socialization, healthy family interaction, and intentional goal setting. His more encompassing objective was to help people rid themselves of insecurities and discover a purposeful self.[15]

Every modern understanding of emotional health and intelligence—including, of course, my own—has been challenged, influenced, or impacted by the foundations laid by pioneers like these and others. Now let's turn our attention to how emotional skills have impacted the world of modern leadership.

The Entry of Emotion into Modern Leadership

I'll get more specific later in the book about the exact way emotional development impacts and empowers leadership. Culture-building, performance-enhancement, job-retention, and expression-management are just a few. For now, I want to simply tease you with a few of the many voices who have convinced me to invest more attention in the emotional growth of our leaders and teams, beginning with this history lesson from the book *Emotional Development and Emotional Intelligence*.

> Experts in psychology and education have long viewed thinking and reason as polar opposites—*reason* on the one hand, and *passion* on the other. And emotion, often labeled as chaotic, haphazard, and immature, has not traditionally been seen as assisting reason.
>
> All that changed in 1990, when Peter Salovey and John D. Mayer coined the term *emotional intelligence*

as a challenge to the belief that intelligence is not based on processing emotion-laded information. Salovey and Mayer defined emotional intelligence as the ability to monitor one's own and others' feelings and emotions, to discriminate among them, and to use this information to guide one's thinking and action.[16]

Jumping forward to 2010, the TED talk "The Power of Vulnerability" propelled famed researcher Brené Brown onto the world stage. With over fifty million views, this particular presentation normalized talk of emotional content and made it acceptable, savvy even, to weave words like "shame" and "empathy" into business conversations.

"I've spent twenty years studying courage, vulnerability, shame, and empathy," Brown reports, "and I recently completed a seven-year study on brave leadership. The goal of [my book] *Dare to Lead* is to share everything we've learned about taking off the armor and showing up as leaders in a skills-based and actionable playbook."[17]

Brown's research concludes with three key takeaways that no effective leader can afford to ignore:

1. You can't get to courage without rumbling with vulnerability.
2. Self-awareness and self-love matter. Who we are is how we lead.
3. Courage is contagious.

Brené Brown's years of research remind us that you can't expect to be a great leader if all you know is how to *do*. You'll have to take intentional steps to deepen your *be*-game. Who you are at the core will either empower or hamstring your leadership. Despite how unassailable this truth is becoming through research and common sense, I'm still amazed at how aggressively resistant leaders and organizations can be when it comes to changing their developmental priorities with their people.

Do you want to be more courageous? Do you want your organization to be more courageous in the marketplace? If the answer is yes, then it's time to shed the armor that has shielded you from the "threat" of growth and kept you mired in old, broken mindsets.

Backed by decades of research, Yale Center for Emotional Intelligence director Marc Brackett makes a bold declaration for including emotions at work. "The evidence is clear: Businesses that wish to remain relevant and competitive in the workplace can't ignore the power of emotions." He does caution, however, that "if employees are faking the good feelings without actually feeling them, the impact on the customer is lost."[18]

Emotional investment is not a manipulation tactic to generate more sales. While high EQ skills can increase sales, they must be undergirded with genuine authenticity to have long-term benefits. Employees who are given the freedom to be completely human will be more likely to connect genuinely with their customers and create trusting relationships. This is the special sauce that anchors all great companies.

In her book *Emotional Intelligence for Sales Success*, Colleen Stanley makes a business case for emotional intelligence when she outlines some bottom-line impacts using three examples:

- In a 1996 U.S. Air Force study, 1,500 recruiters were tested to discover common EI traits among those who achieved 100 percent of their quota. By duplicating those EI traits, retention rates increased 92 percent, saving in excess of $2.7 million.
- In a pioneering EQ project, American Express put a group of financial advisors through a three-day emotional awareness training. The following year, those trainees' sales exceeded untrained colleagues by two percent, resulting in millions of extra earnings.
- At L'Oréal, twenty-eight sales agents selected on the basis of certain emotional competencies sold on average $91,370 more than salespeople not tested, for a net revenue increase of $2,558,360.[19]

I am inspired by companies that are willing to invest in humanized ways of doing business. Clients like Ashley Furniture, DSG, Atlas Real Estate, GEODIS, MLS, and the Collective are just a few of those I get to work with at Transformed Leader—companies that are putting their money, energy, and commitment where their people are. These businesses are ahead of the curve, fighting for a better new normal. Fighting for heart.

WHY ARE WE STILL
LEAVING THE BEST
PARTS OF OURSELVES
BEHIND WHEN WE
GO TO WORK?

Is it easy? Of course not. But we are all showing up and fighting in our own ways for a better tomorrow. The majority of modern workers across the world still slog through bureaucratic, emotionally bankrupt halls of dimly lit cubicles where the incarcerated try to urge the clock faster with pleading looks. Frederic Laloux writes tellingly, "Organizations are places for the most part, in the true sense of the word, soulless places—places inhospitable to our deeper selfhood and to the secret longings of our soul."[20] Why are we still leaving the best parts of ourselves behind when we go to work?

When it comes to the intersection of emotional intelligence and leadership development, no other name is as recognizable and respected as bestselling author and researcher Daniel Goleman. He believes that EQ is twice as valuable as any other competency in determining outstanding leadership.

It's not that IQ and technical skills are irrelevant. They do matter, but mainly as 'threshold capabilities'; that is, they are entry-level requirements for executive positions. But my research, along with other recent studies, clearly shows that emotional intelligence is the *sine qua non* of leadership. Without it, a person can have the best training in the world, an incisive, analytical mind, and an endless supply of smart ideas, but he still won't make a great leader.[21]

Goleman has boldly led the field, working tirelessly to examine and aggregate the relationships between heart-engagement and leadership performance. If you are a business leader, and hope to be a better one, but have yet to establish a handle on the essentiality of emotional capacity to organizational success, you need to find some people in this field to follow as soon as possible. We don't all have to be experts, but we do need to at least be aware.

While I personally focus on deepening the heart and soul of organizations, I know that I must also remain somewhat current in the auxiliary fields of strategic planning, operational efficiencies, corporate structures, best practice policies, etc. Having a leadership focus is vital, but we can't lose a holistic perspective of the entire landscape. Find researchers, authors, conferences, books, coaches, and mentors outside of your go-to leadership structures.

In fact, our next topic takes us directly into one of these larger perspectives.

The Human Operating System

My first book, a collaboration with my partner Jack Nicholson, is titled *The Human Operating System: Recovering the Heart and Soul of Your Leadership*. The book you're reading now fits squarely within this larger paradigm. As you know, the operating system of any electronic device is the fundamental architecture upon which the applications run. So whether it's iOS, Android, or Windows, every function of the device depends upon, is directed by, and is limited by its underlying framework. This is also true of humans.

We, too, have a foundational architecture, and one of the most enduring ways to describe human architecture is with four simple words that describe a very complex reality: *heart, soul, mind*, and *strength*. Elementary words, perhaps, but effective nonetheless. Philosophers, scientists, and religious leaders have used these words for millennia to probe the intricacies of the human condition.

In our book, we describe these "quadrants" and the role each plays to enrich our lives. We also offer a system for recognizing our starter quadrant, actively developing the integration of all four, and harnessing heart and soul in particular to empower modern leadership. So while I won't try to repeat the insights from that book in this one, I do want to contextualize our current topic within that larger perspective. For starters, let's run a quick excerpt from our book to showcase the four quadrants that comprise the Human Operating System, or HOS for short.

Strength. This quadrant describes the *sensory center* of our being—that part of us that allows us to absorb the tactile data around us and convert that information into action. From this space we experience and engage the physical world, gathering resources and adopting behaviors for accomplishing goals. This quadrant is anchored in our bodies and as such, is distinct from the other three internal dimensions of self.

Mind. This dimension describes the *strategic center* of our being—that part of us that organizes and structures our inner and outer worlds into intelligible systems. From this space we seek to understand reality and sort it into logical connections that make sense and provide coherence and safety, for ourselves and others. From the mind, we build and attach ourselves to theories and truths that provide a container to hold our way of being in the world.

Soul. This is the *meaning center* of our being—the part of us that seeks to make sense of our lives, our stories, and our purpose in the world. From this space we dream, imagine, and create. We cast a vision for our lives, our families, and our business enterprises and then inspire ourselves and others toward that desired future.

Heart. This quadrant describes the *emotive center* of our being—that part of us that feels, values, wills, and connects with others. From this inner space we discover who we are, what we want, and who we want to relate to. From this dimension, we build social constructs, find our tribe, and build a life with and for others.

Effective leaders are those who are willing and able to learn the language of each quadrant and then harness the unique contributions of each quadrant into the various facets of their lives.

The quadrants are really not unlike foreign languages, and learning a new one requires mastering the fundamentals of vocabulary, syntax, and grammar. Each "language" brings its own unique perspective on reality, and the transformational leader is one who can learn each fluently.[22]

Jack and I developed the HOS as a metaphor for describing the ultimate realities of how people, leaders, and relational systems function. When the four quadrants are combined strategically, they form a powerful force to help leaders wisely engage structural and systemic problems. It is a simple, elegant way to understand complex issues and the relational dynamics that motivate organizations to be healthy and productive. *Fighting for Heart* and The Heart-Engaged System, as you might imagine, are a deep dive into the heart quadrant. As you invest in this arena, you might also enjoy looking to the larger HOS model to better activate and integrate the whole package.

Speaking of integration, Jack and I have come to believe that training can equip leaders, but it is *integration that opens the possibility for transformation.* Integration calls for the collaboration of heart, soul, mind, and strength, inviting someone to trade idealism for more authenticity. I will deepen this concept in the next chapter where I invite you to take an integrative step toward becoming a more emotionally engaged leader.

My hope is to present a case compelling enough to move you to dive deep into the work it will take to become Heart-Engaged. Heart alone will not be enough to be exceptional in your work, but it is central, and you can't be fully alive without it. Consider this book an "application" that runs on the Human Operating System.

Getting Into the Gym

I introduced a gym analogy earlier: You have to practice feelings; you can't just learn about them. You can't just buy a membership. You ultimately have to make the choice to start going. Consider heart-work "legs day" at the gym. Without accountability, I somehow find myself spending a significant amount of time in the outdoor jacuzzi. And when I find the inspiration to make it onto the gym floor, I gravitate toward working on my biceps and triceps, the "glamour muscles." They make you *look* strong, but are you really?

Jared, my fitness guide (hired to take me to workout places I won't go myself), will tell you that without a strong core, fitness is a pipe dream. Next in line are legs and back. Legs are the biggest muscle group in the body, yet many gym rats take them for granted and avoid this crucial investment.

And that's how most leaders treat their heart intelligence. Some never make it to the developmental gym at all, while others get there and spend too much time on sparkles and spicy. Wise leaders focus on the fundamentals without neglecting the whole. My hope is that, between this book and my last one, you'll have access to both.

It's also honest to acknowledge that we all experience resistance to the things that are good for us, whether it be exercising our physical hearts or our metaphysical hearts. My research found that there are six common resistances that keep leaders from investing in their emotional growth. See if you recognize any of these:

1. Self-protection against social shame, pressure, or judgments for being "emotional."

2. Holding a belief that leaders should not be distracted by emotions.
3. Avoiding emotions feels easier, safer, and more manageable.
4. Lack of emotional modeling growing up.
5. Ignorance of any other way than performing and producing.
6. Not justifying the time and money to prioritize emotional development.[23]

These resistances are deeply understandable and deeply destructive. Which ones can you relate to in your life and leadership? Let's dismantle them together and find a new narrative to carry us into a new future.

I'd like to close this chapter with a personal experience that has molded my journey with brain science, personally and professionally. A few years ago, I sustained a neck injury that released rogue blood clots into my bloodstream and landed in my brain. I had a stroke. Doctors found five points of trauma on my brain from the event. The good news was I could finally prove I had a brain; the bad news was that the trauma had damaged a few things, and I have been working through my recovery ever since.

From the scan data, the doctor could see that much of the trauma was located near the parts of my brain that impact eyesight, emotion, and memory. Scientific discussion aside, my subjective experience (confirmed by family and friends) is that these brain injuries impacted my emotional systems, including my feelings, facial expressions, and emotional regulation.

It was tough to achieve eye focus for a couple of months. Three days of memory vanished while stuck in a two-minute loop in the hospital. And I have struggled with emotional dysregulation and saturation. There are still times when the slightest background music can overwhelm my concentration and disrupt my presence at the dinner table.

For months after my stroke, my words would not match my facial expressions. I could say something encouraging yet my expressions appeared dark. I found myself having to reassure people that, despite my frowning intensity, I was trying to communicate positive intent. "Rob, is what you are saying a good thing or a bad thing? I can't tell. Your face says one thing and your words another."

As a result of this experience, I've been able to conduct a little up-close-and-personal research on the extensive connections between mind and heart, and I've come away with an inescapable conviction: *wholeness of heart lies at the crux of wholeness of life.* And in this next chapter, we're going to start learning how to get there. While you may not have had a stroke, I am certain you can identify and relate with a trauma or tragedy of your own. What is your stroke? Is it a divorce, a diagnosis, a bankruptcy, the death of a loved one, a rejection from a parent or child? Life has a way of forcing all of us to face big things sooner or later.

CHAPTER 3

CATCHING UP TO YOURSELF

Learn to know yourself [and]
search realistically and
regularly the processes of
your own mind and feelings.
NELSON MANDELA

MY WIFE NATALIE shares some of her story here.

> *If you had asked me a few years ago, "Who are you?"*
> *I could have given you an answer. But I would give*
> *you a pretty different one today. I've learned a lot*
> *about the self embedded in this body over time. The*
> *deconstructive challenges of chronic illness, midlife*
> *transitions, and family complexities have made it*
> *challenging to know the real me, but I am pushing*
> *forward, somewhat courageously, to understand and*
> *live in my true self more fully.*

I had perfected certain coping mechanisms over time—specifically, the ability to detach from painful or threatening situations with apparent ease and the ability to dismiss my desires, even my feelings entirely, in order to take the path of least resistance. With little sense of my true self, I was able to push through the hardest and worst of difficulties. But this came at a cost. A hard diagnosis from a doctor, yet I left the treatment plan on the table. A painful body, yet I marched on. Who has time and bandwidth to pay attention to the inner life when there is stuff to avoid, stuff to do, and people to take care of?

I remember the first time a woman named Michelle guided me through a mindfulness practice. I was lying on the floor of her office throbbing with agony, while she tried to get me to focus directly on the pain. "Just notice it," she said. As if I could ignore it. "Allow the pain to exist, but don't let it take you over."

If you have ever struggled with chronic mental, emotional, or physical pain, you will know how denial and distraction temporarily soothe the ruthless agitations. Temporarily. Rather than denial, though, Michelle was inviting me to stop resisting the pain and actually have a conversation with it. She was inviting integration rather than dissociation. Maybe even a first step toward acceptance.

When it comes to the four quadrants advocated in my husband Rob's work, I find it somewhat easy to *engage my mind and soul. But heart and body have been harder for me to access: my body, for obvious reasons, and my heart, well, because I didn't know what to do with feelings. And the interplay between physical feelings and emotional feelings was often too tangled to parse out.*

Gradually, my well-honed adaptations began to loosen their grip, and I started to have choices. With a fresh commitment to intentional self-awareness and discovery, I have taken meaningful steps to get in touch with my heart, and I've begun to name, honor, and respect what I find there.

Over time and with many encouraging voices, I learned how to catch up to myself. How to move beyond the screaming parts of myself and listen to the quieter voices that are also genuinely me. How to let body, soul, mind, and heart exist and be heard with their particular tone and truth. There is rarely a truce between those four, but I am learning that being more connected to all the parts brings more integration with my faith, myself, and others. So, I work hard to keep showing up despite the challenges.

I'm learning to be more compassionate with myself as I get out of bed each day to live, parent, work, and love while in pain, without losing my sense of identity. It's not easy, but the consistent practice of catching up with myself has made me a more whole, healthy person. And for that, I am deeply grateful.

There is significant consensus across bodies of research in the leadership industry that affirms self-awareness as the single most powerful competency for a leader to develop. The *Harvard Business Review* reports that "when the 75 members of Stanford Graduate School of Business Advisory Council were asked to recommend the most important capabilities for leaders to develop, their answer was nearly unanimous: self-awareness."[24] Without this vital quality, we are the blind leading the blind.

Natalie's story reminds us of both the beauty and the pain that come from the concerted effort to know oneself. Most people would say they want to be more self-aware, to see themselves more clearly, but several forces collude to obstruct that goal as mentioned in chapter one: denial, distraction, and determination (the Three Ds of survival). Those are the biggies.

In the world of commerce, you may want to throw in a few more: lack of understanding, lack of training, and lack of experience. The priority to know and cultivate a leader's sense of self sounds like crazy talk in a world where spreadsheets, products, and customer acquisitions reign supreme.

In my consulting practice, we help seasoned leaders unpack parts of themselves that have been stuffed into the closet, rarely, if ever, to see the light of day. When I repeat what they say about themselves, their eyes open wide in shock, scarcely believing their own revelations of the Self. Simple, but powerful.

What is the ROI for all this feelings stuff? You may find these top outcomes, provided by those who have entered the EQ work with us, helpful. This is what happens when people engage their hearts.

1. They became more open, honest, accepting, accountable, curious, and confident with their emotions.
2. They experienced more connection with themselves and others.
3. They gained a new ability to verbalize and articulate their emotions.
4. They gained the awareness and ability to identify the feelings of others.
5. They started relating to others in a different, more positive way.
6. They found tools and resources for growing their emotional capacity.
7. They discovered a safe place to process, practice, and push through obstacles.
8. They became better able to model healthy emotions for others.
9. They disrupted outside existing relationships (both positively and negatively).
10. They were able to rewrite previously held mindsets by normalizing emotions.[25]

What if the Heart-Engaged EQ System could guide you towards some of these outcomes in your own life and leadership? You will only know what you only know unless you intentionally search for more. There is always a further journey, but only the courageous are willing (or forced at times) to "pull the thread on the sweater" and see what happens. Or to follow Lewis Carroll's timeless query, "Just how far down the rabbit hole are you willing to go?" Or the red pill in *The Matrix*. You get the point.

Step 1: Catch Up to Yourself

Over the first couple of chapters, I laid a foundation for what feelings are, the different attitudes people carry about feelings, and the rich contributions being made to this field of study that highlight their value in life and leadership. Now I want to start giving you some tools for working practically and skillfully with your Heart.

At Transformed Leader, I have drawn upon our years of collective experience to create a powerful model I call the Heart-Engaged EQ System. It's a map to the "rabbit hole," so to speak, that will help you understand and harness the latent authority of your emotional intelligence to build healthy relationships with yourself, your family, and your work colleagues.

Step 1 in the Heart-Engaged process begins with four actions with each directed to one of the four quadrants of the Heart: I have divided the Heart into four quadrants that reflect the architecture of the Human Operating System (Heart, Soul, Mind, and Strength). But here I apply those dynamics specifically and directly to the Heart itself: *Strength of Heart*, *Mind of Heart*, *Soul of Heart*, and *Heart of Heart*.

In other words, I want to parse out four aspects of the emotional life: the essential *meaning* of our emotions (soul), the personal *experience* of our emotions (heart), the chief *influencers* of our emotions (mind), and the primary *effects* of our emotions (strength). This will become increasingly clear as we engage in the work itself. And the work begins with catching up to yourself.

mind of heart
LOGICAL EQ

strength of heart
PRACTICAL EQ

notice your
THOUGHTS

connect to your
BODY

refresh your
MEANING

identify your
FEELINGS

PURPOSE EQ
soul of heart

SOCIAL EQ
heart of heart

Connect to Your Body

This is a great starting point. Either by yourself or with your team, take a few deep, conscious breaths and engage the *strength of your heart*. This simple act grounds us in our physicality, which is the essential container we inhabit. Slow down long enough to recognize how your body may be carrying the stress, excitement, anticipation, or weight of your life.

Listen to your body. Are you in it? Are you aware of pain or tension? Peace and relaxation? What is it wanting to tell you right now? If the different parts of your body could speak, what would they say?

One of the deductions I have made from the research of Bessel van der Kolk, specifically in his book *The Body Keeps the Score*, is that your body will, in time, physically manifest what your heart and soul refuse to face. Emotional conditions like loneliness, anxiety, and depression are known to be initiators and catalysts for many types of physical ailments that present themselves in the body. Learning how to assess your physical body will invite the opportunity to become more self-aware as you learn how your insides and outsides are responding or reacting with or against each other.

Consciously connect with your body. Welcome it to the party, both the weak parts and the strong parts. Reserve judgment and simply be present. Cultivate grace and gratitude. Accept this body that is serving to house you. Choose to enter this day with attunement and integration rather than ignorance and dissociation.

Notice Your Thoughts

Is your mind calm, clear, and connected, or is it scattered, chaotic, and anxious? Are you bouncing around or focused? Are your thoughts rigid and judgmental, or are they curious and creative? These questions call your thoughts to attention and accountability. There is no right answer, by the way, just the assignment to notice and observe the *mind of your heart*. Thoughts carry a lot of influence over our behaviors, feelings, and purpose. And because we tend to over-rely on them, they are highly subject to getting hijacked by the data overload of life and leadership. "Monkey mind" is a common experience, and it's a serious impediment to showing up as our best selves. For the mind to serve us at full capacity, it must be quiet rather than chaotic. Multi-tasking is not only a myth (we never actually focus on more than one item at a time), but an enemy to the priority of presence.

Learning to notice your thoughts, to offer them a voice, and to let go of the ones not serving you at the moment is a great step toward becoming a mature, integrated man or woman.

Refresh Your Meaning

Turning to the *soul of your heart*, I encourage leaders to refresh their sense of purpose and meaning. Bring your "why" back to the forefront of your attention in this step so you can lead from a sharper focus of personal vision and mission.

If you become aware of a lack of clarity around your meaning, don't worry. This truth is equally important. Far better to notice a lack of clarity and attend to this need than to blunder ahead and lead blindly.

The role of the soul is to ground our activity in meaning. This capacity assigns value to our actions and keeps us from running on the proverbial gerbil wheel, exerting great effort but not moving forward toward our true goals. In fact, this entire Step 1 is a soul-based activity that reattaches and reanchors us to reality.

Identify Your Feelings

Now we come to the *heart of the heart*, and this will be the deeper focus of Step 2. For now, having connected to your body, noticed your thoughts, and refreshed your meaning, you can make a quick pass through the heart to notice any loud, demanding, or flooded feelings taking up a lot of space in the room. You don't need to fix them or manage them, just recognize them. I promise you, doing even this simple step will qualify you as the most self-aware person in the room— and set you up for a seamless transition into Step 2, which we'll describe in the next chapter.

Congratulations! You've just completed Step 1 of the Heart-Engaged EQ System. These four check-in points are deeply centering, and you can tap into their wisdom to recalibrate yourself in any challenging situation or conversation. These parts of yourself have information to continually shape you as a heart-smart leader.

This is part of becoming "multi-lingual" in the languages of emotional intelligence. Without the data of all four quadrants, we are left rudderless, with no reality checks to guide our interactions. This is what we experience when we're tossed, driven, or blown around by whomever and whatever shouts the loudest in any particular moment. You can still get stuff done without a grounded self (what we will shortly describe as the Core Self), but quality and character pay the price.

Having circled the quadrants, you have now done a quick but meaningful check-in with these four parts of yourself and identified both positive and negative influences. Remember to withhold judgment and practice being a gracious observer of yourself. Over time, this step will dramatically fuel a profound sense of self-awareness.

Just How Self-Aware Are You?

"According to research by organizational psychologist Tasha Eurich, 95% of people think they're self-aware, but only ten to fifteen percent actually are, and that can pose problems for your employees. Working with colleagues who aren't self-aware can cut a team's success in half and, according to Eurich's research, lead to increased stress and decreased motivation."[26]

That sounds about right to me. We *believe* we are self-aware but are not as aware as we think. And of course, we don't know what we don't know. It's similar to how almost everyone thinks he or she is a great driver; it's all those other nuts out there on the road who cause the problems. Yeah, right.

Lauren Landry writes for the Harvard Business School and continues this thought: "In order to bring out the best in others, you first need to bring out the best in yourself, which is where self-awareness comes into play. One easy way to assess your self-awareness is by completing 360-degree feedback, in which you evaluate your performance and then match it up against the opinions of your boss, peers, and direct reports. Through this process, you'll gain insights into your own behavior and discover how you're perceived in the organization."[27]

I have come to believe that self-awareness is both the most desirable attribute of our human potential but also the most difficult to welcome and cultivate. Looking into the mirror that others hold up for us can help us tune in to reality and obtain priceless information for our leadership. But it requires great courage. We have to push through the initial sting of recognizing our shortcomings so we can then push into new territory of skill, effectiveness, and satisfaction.

Are you up for it?

I was running a self-awareness check with a group of executives a while back, and they were enthusiastic. They had just run through a sheet of words with specific feelings listed (similar to what we will do in Step 2). This exercise invited them outside the banalities of our common word-play: "How's it going? Doing great. How are you?" And even though this word list pushed them into a greater level of

SELF-AWARENESS
IS BOTH THE MOST DESIRABLE
ATTRIBUTE OF OUR HUMAN
POTENTIAL BUT ALSO THE MOST
DIFFICULT TO WELCOME AND
CULTIVATE.

self-awareness, they seemed relatively comfortable with the initial invitation.

One leader confidently declared himself "naturally self-aware" and completely at ease with the exercise and the feelings that followed. *Fair enough*, I thought. *Let's keep pushing the envelope to see if he's ready for more.*

"Gentlemen, you did a fantastic job of learning to say out loud what is going on inside of you. Connecting these dots is part of growing a strong internal core, sturdy enough to be a person of character and significance. And . . . this is just the beginning. The first steps to learning a new language." I paused, and then asked, "Does anyone want an assignment that will take you a level up from what we safely did today? The invitation will be to expand your self-awareness and push you further than what you can see and accomplish by yourself."

"For sure," a few leaders responded, rising to take the challenge.

"Okay, great. Your assignment is to find a quiet moment in the next few days at home with your spouse or significant other. Sit down together and ask them what it feels like to be in relationship with you. And, they have a full uninterrupted sixty minutes at least." I allowed that mental scene to sink in for a moment.

"You will likely need to ask the same question at least three to five different ways. Their first few answers will be cautious. They'll be caught off guard by your invitation and need to see how you respond to their initial feedback; they're going to test the waters to see how safe it is to share deeper experiences

CATCHING UP TO YOURSELF

and truths, to tell you what it feels like to be them . . . with you. And here are the rules: *You can only listen.* You can't respond with explanations, arguments, or punishments. You can only respond with 'Tell me more' and 'Thank you for sharing.' That's it."

The room tittered with nervous laughter and subdued comments to the tune of, "Um no, not sure I want to hear that. Sounds dangerous to me. Talk about opening up a can of worms."

"If you're feeling brave," I continued, "You can do the same with each of your children, asking them individually how they experience you as a parent. The goal is to understand what they see in and about you that you don't see for yourself. This is not for the faint of heart; it's for the courageous of heart. And those who want to grow their capacity of heart."

Indeed, *what else is there to know about ourselves?* Probably an immense amount. Probably a few things we'd rather not know. Because then we would be responsible for them. And while ignorance and denial sometimes feel like bliss, if we're creating difficulties for ourselves and others, wouldn't we want to know that? Doesn't part of us want to rise to be the best version of ourselves? If so, that requires taking the risk to ask and listen. The pathway to a robust self-awareness involves holding the tension that we are both better than we often believe and at the same time more fallible than we think. Polarize at either end and you will be overrun by shame or by pride; neither offers an accurate perspective of your true essence.

Increasing self-awareness is best done by inviting safe, trusted people who love and care about you to share how they experience you. Their experiences and feedback may not always be completely accurate, but they will offer you priceless data about how you show up in the world and how others may feel about you in totality.

Self-awareness is about cultivating a conscious knowledge of one's essence. How that essence is expressed through things such as character, feelings, motives, actions, and desires. These are the attributes we must understand and deepen if we hope to become more transformational in personal and professional spheres. The wider your influence, the more vital it is for people to experience you as trustworthy, genuine, and authentic . . . and for you to actually *be* those things.

If there is one absolutely essential quality to becoming Heart-Engaged, it would be this one. Emotional intelligence is *more* than self-awareness, but it's not less. Aspiring humans that seek to engage fully with themselves and with those around them must cultivate this quality. And as they do, they will become more skillful at communication, teamwork, problem-solving, stress management, and decision making.

Heart-Engaged leaders will evidence congruency between what they say and do. What others experience on the outside will become increasingly consistent with the essential core of who they are on the inside. So, here's a question: *What are you and your company doing to invest in these areas of growth and development?*

"People who have a high degree of self-awareness," Daniel Goleman says, "recognize how their feelings affect them, other people, and their job performance. Thus, a self-aware person who knows that tight deadlines bring out the worst in him plans his time carefully and gets his work done well in advance. Another person with high self-awareness will be able to work with a demanding client. She will understand the client's impact on her moods and the deeper reasons for her frustration."[28] Solid insights from the industry's best-known spokesperson in the EQ space.

The Johari Window

The Johari window is a legendary tool for demonstrating four key facets to self-awareness and inviting us to explore each. Before we get started, though, I bet you're wondering what's the story on this person Johari? Sounds Persian or something. The entertaining answer is that the name is actually a blend of the two American psychologists who designed the model, Joseph and Harry.

What I love about this model is how it helps us demystify this idea of our Core Self. It also invites us to consider the shadows, avoidances, and ignorance we work hard to manage. All healthy leaders are aware there are things they know and things they don't know about themselves. They are also conscious of the reality that others know things and don't know things about them too.

The four "panes" of the window represent the awareness

of an individual regarding behaviors, feelings, and motivations. In any interaction between people, it's a graphic way to describe who knows what. This is not about knowing peripheral data: what time it is or where the car is parked. It's about knowing what's going on inside an individual. What a person is doing, why he or she is doing it, and the emotional content involved.

The matrix, as you can see, has two axes: the two vertical columns represent what is *known and not known to the self.* The two horizontal lines represent what is known and not known to others. This gives us four possible combinations, which are labelled Open, Blind, Hidden, and Unknown.

	KNOWN TO SELF	**NOT KNOWN TO SELF**
KNOWN TO OTHERS	*Open*	*Blind*
NOT KNOWN TO OTHERS	*Hidden*	*Unknown*

The **Open Self** represents those behaviors, feelings, and motivations that are known to you *and* known to others. This is a reasonably comfortable space because everybody's in the know in this particular exchange. The windowpane is fully transparent.

You also have a **Blind Self**, which is less comfortable, but you only know it abstractly. You know theoretically that others know things about you that you don't. It's a one-way window, so to speak: Others can see in, but you can't see out. *Remember the exercise about asking your spouse or kids how they experience you?* That exercise is designed precisely to bring light into your blind spots, thus moving that data from the Blind windowpane to the Open windowpane.

Going beneath the line you have the **Hidden Self**. This category represents the parts of who you are that you are well aware of but work hard to ensure no one else sees. This is perhaps the most uncomfortable windowpane, and we have words like *shame*, *guilt*, and *loneliness* to describe its contents. We raise a façade to project an ideal version of who we are to others, carefully shielding ourselves from the avoided, forbidden, or shaded parts that feel unacceptable in the land of the living. This windowpane holds the areas that usually require some form of "shadow work" for those seeking personal freedom and healthy boundaries. Shadow work is an approach to bring more of our hidden or unknown parts into the light so they can be considered, integrated, and even healed.

Finally, the **Unknown Self** represents those behaviors, feelings, and motivations that neither you nor the person you're interacting with recognize. This space is quite comfortable since no one sees it at all; the pane is "frosted" in our visual. Opaque.

Now let's try to apply the model to a real-world scenario. Let's say you and your work assistant are collaborating on a presentation for next week. You both know a slideshow is involved because you're both contributing graphs and images. The Open windowpane. You and your assistant both also know you're feeling pressure to get it done before you leave town for vacation tomorrow. Again, this is the Open category. Both behavior and feelings are understood by both.

But your assistant is observant. He knows that when you get upset or fear failure, you start raising your voice. It's instinctive for you; you don't even notice you're doing it. But he does. And he decides to retreat to his own office. A classic Blind spot. Windowpane two. You're behaving in ways you can't see but others can.

However, your assistant does *not* know that you had a fight with your spouse this morning, and that's the real reason you're being snarky. And you want your personal life to stay that way. Heaven forbid your assistant, or the new boss would have cause to doubt your competence across all areas of life, personal and professional. Bottom left windowpane: the Hidden Self. Both the feelings and the motivations are known to you and being managed by you, but not known to others.

But there's another option here, maybe an even more likely scenario. You might be tense and impatient with your assistant because of that morning's fight with your spouse but you don't even know why you're swearing under your breath. You think it's because of time pressure, but it's really because you feel misunderstood by your spouse. You're not in contact with your "insides" in this situation, which means you have not yet acquired enough self-awareness to make the connection between the feelings of this personal conflict with the pressures of your professional deadline. Neither you nor your assistant sees it. This is the Unknown Self.

Wow! So many possibilities. So many situations. In just minutes, we might jump between all four panes in the Johari Window several times. In fact, at any given moment, there is an untold amount of personal content piled up in all four windowpanes representing a host of different behaviors, feelings, and motivations. If you look at it in the aggregate, it's overwhelming. But if you look at one behavior, one feeling, or one motivation at a time, it's profoundly insightful.

We're talking about self-awareness, about noticing the whole Self. And the Johari Window gives us four powerful positions to differentiate what's going on with the Self right now. Can you imagine pausing in the copy room, as you're copying handouts for that presentation, taking a few deep breaths and asking yourself, "Okay, what's going on inside me right now? What's open, blind, hidden, or unknown in this situation? What are my motivations? What can I do to widen the window and enlarge my perspectives? What feedback do I need? What behaviors do I need to take responsibility for?"

This is the kind of opportunity we have daily—to lead with or without emotional intelligence. With or without connection to our Hearts. With or without synergy in our teams. With or without effectiveness. Grounded in our truest selves or adrift in projections. The stakes are high, and we know we're meant for more, so let's keep leaning into the potential of the Heart-Engaged EQ System.

Dialing in Your Core-Self

Before we move to Step 2, let's push Step 1 forward a bit further. First, let's make sure we know what we're talking about when we discuss the Self, and second, let's look at four strategic levels of awareness that can be achieved from taking a lifelong journey of dedicated laps around the heart.

Susan David writes, "A malleable sense of self is the cornerstone of emotional agility. People who have a growth mindset and who see themselves as agents in their own lives are more open to new experiences, more willing to take risks, more persistent, and more resilient in rebounding from failure. They are less likely to mindlessly conform to others' wishes and values and more likely to be creative and entrepreneurial."[29]

A "malleable sense of self"—what is that? I think it's several things. It's a self-concept that hasn't grown stiff and rigid; instead, it seeks to evolve toward its true design. It's also a Self that realizes its propensity to wear masks—idealized versions of the Self that, left unchecked, become a caricature of the truth and diminish our true potential. We like to use the term Core Self to describe this agile, adaptable, growing, honest version of ourselves.

On this journey to knowing—and living from—the Core Self, we're uncovering various hazards: self-ignorance (well framed by the Johari Window), the idealized self, created to please and impress, the fossilized self that resists change, and the shadow self that responds to pressures with fight, flight, or freeze.

Father Richard Rohr describes the challenges this way:

The more we have cultivated and protected a chosen persona, the more shadow work we will need to do. Therefore, we need to be especially careful of clinging to any idealized role or self-image, like that of minister, mother, doctor, nice person, professor, moral believer, or president of this or that. These are huge personas to live up to, and they trap many people in lifelong delusion that the role is who they are or who they are only allowed to be.

Beneath all these self-states of adaptation and personality, I believe there is a Core Self that has receptivity at its heart. Some researchers call this core *ipseity*, from the Latin word *ipse*, meaning "itself." This is the essence that must come forth over our life journey. Rohr encourages us "to find who we are, [what] the Zen masters call *the face we had before we were born*. This self cannot die, lives forever, and is our True Self."[30]

Revisiting Susan David's quote, she talks about emotional agility as being able to see yourself with agency or power. It raises the question: *Are you living your life or is your life living you?* Are you able to occupy your life from the inside but also observe it from the outside? Does the buck stop with your

ARE YOU LIVING
YOUR LIFE
OR IS YOUR LIFE
LIVING YOU?

willpower, intellect, and morality, or does it instead stop with your Core Self?

This is a subtle but essential difference. I believe very few people are truly living their lives as an outward expression of their inward reality.

The Core Self is a deeper, more authentic, more enduring reality than the Self expressed in actions, feelings, and thoughts. Those expressions of body, heart, and mind are vital, but they are also volatile and changing day by day. Underneath those vacillations, however, is something more essential. You can call it your essence. I call it the Core Self.

Sometimes these esoteric realities are best recognized in a real-world scenario. I'm attending a big, busy, noisy birthday party for a friend. Seeking a quiet reset, I sneak away to another room, only to find another guy I've not met fidgeting on his phone. Maybe he had the same idea as me, I thought, just needing to get away from the action for a moment.

"Hi," I said and plopped down on the neighboring couch to catch up to myself—to take a lap around the four Heart-quadrants and see what was going on underneath the noise.

Either to cut the awkwardness or to make small talk, he pitches the common, "What do you do?"

Honestly, I was thrown off, given I had found this room to recover. And now I felt the pressure to make the case for who I am by sharing what I do. In this context, I felt wearied by trying to project my internal personhood by sharing my external vocation.

"What do I do? I drink wine," I answered, trying to escape

the inquiry lightheartedly. And I take a sip from my glass. It's a dodge I learned from a wise man named Jerry. Caught off guard but feeling the need to complete the liturgy, he pressed forward.

"No, I mean what do you do for a living?"

Again, I felt my heels digging in. I was ornery and tired, having escaped to this quiet spot desperately needing to recoup.

"I chase life for a living" was my next sidestep.

The awkward exchange was brief, clearly because of my unruly social etiquette with an innocent bystander. But it's a telling view on the different layers of self we tend to occupy, from the most idealistic identities of where we land on the organizational chart to our truer identities found in our desires and motivations, and to the almost indefinable identity of the Core Self.

All leaders need times and places to retreat from the crowd and catch up to themselves. That's why Step 1 is where Heart-Engaged people begin. Preferably, the catch-up is done prior to social events, but during and afterward can be helpful as well. In a world where what you do defines who you are, we have to embrace the concept of Core Self leadership. We must perceive the opportunities to plunge beneath the waterline of job title and ask people who they are.

How much more inviting it could have been for that gentleman to say something like, "Tell me about yourself" or "Who are you and how do you fit at this party?" Either of those would have been congruent and connecting, and I would have warmed to the invitation.

Whether the setting is social or business, emotionally intelligent leaders develop the capacity to go beyond externals to internals. Beyond niceties to something meaningful. If you pull on the thread of the self-awareness journey and follow the trail to your core, you'll find yourself living and relating from your truer Self while giving other people permission to live from theirs.

I call this Formance Leadership. Your *form* inspires and catalyzes how you and others *perform*. Performance Leadership is a hot button for most leaders, but the secret sauce for the best leaders comes from cultivating an easy expertise with the Core Self. Simply put, Heart-Engaged leaders flow from a place of well-mapped identity. Who they are drives what they do. Emotional intelligence offers a journey of inquiry to discover the stratified layers of your life.

Journey to the Center of Your Self

John Naisbitt, author of the 1982 mega-hit book *Megatrends: Ten New Directions Transforming Our Lives* says, "The most exciting breakthroughs of the twenty-first century will not occur because of technology, but because of an expanding concept of what it means to be human."[31] I think we are watching that prophetic vision play out before our eyes. Both my first book and this one represent efforts to map this very humanity that is expanding in understanding and practice.

So, let's take Step 1 even further before we move on. You know the four heart quadrants and the actions associated with each: *Connect to Your Body, Notice Your Thoughts, Refresh Your Meaning, and Identify Your Feelings.* You've done that.

The first lap of the Catch-Up is designed to help leaders learn how to make contact with their Core Self in the hope that they will grow in self-awareness, becoming individuals who can live and lead with congruency. But making contact with your Core Self is just the start. Let's take a few more laps.

The earth orbits the sun like the rings of a tree track its growth over time. Instead of attempting to achieve your life, you can instead start to live it. One circuit at a time.

"Human consciousness evolves in successive stages," says Frederic Laloux. "There is no wishing away the massive amounts of evidence that backs this reality. The problem is not with the reality of the stages; it is how we view the staircase. We get into trouble when we believe that later stages are 'better' than earlier stages; a more helpful interpretation is that they are more 'complex' ways of dealing with the world."[32]

If you are willing to engage the transformational heart adventure, you will begin to journey toward the center of your being. The four series of laps you can expect or hope to encounter throughout your lifetime are Contact, Communicate, Connect, and finally, Commune. This is called the Four Levels of Emotional Depth. Here's another way of looking at our earlier diagram.

FOUR LEVELS OF EMOTIONAL DEPTH

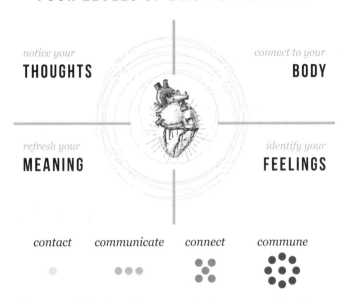

notice your
THOUGHTS

connect to your
BODY

refresh your
MEANING

identify your
FEELINGS

contact	*communicate*	*connect*	*commune*

Contact. The first laps are a holistic scan. It offers you contact with your mind, your body, your heart, and your soul; it opens the door to becoming an emotionally informed person. The first movement toward emotional health is learning to make contact with ourselves, and while seemingly straightforward, very few set out on this journey. Without this initial practice to lay the foundation, it is nearly impossible to go beyond the surface of your everyday life activities.

Making contact with yourself today, perhaps you become aware that you are feeling angry and frustrated with your coworker and think she is incapable of her job, given her confusion with your proposal. And when you get frustrated, you notice your shoulders tighten up. This is an important start to self-awareness. The beginning of the inner journey. I know it seems simple, but you will be surprised how few people are able to slow down and make this first layer of contact.

We call this the Inner Observer—the part of ourselves we train to pay attention to what's actually going on internally rather than just living on autopilot. All four of these laps are ways to strengthen our self-awareness and self-leadership.

Communicate. As you become more comfortable checking in with yourself by taking these laps, in time you will begin to notice Contact leading you to Communicate. As you become more self-aware, you will be able to name what's going on inside of you—first to yourself, and then to others. Naming is a powerful act; it allows you to own your reality. It's a way of coming out of the darkness and stepping into the light. It's a place of freedom.

Let's say you are confronted by someone on your team who feels hurt because you don't make concerted efforts to ask for her input at meetings. Her feelings catch you by surprise, given that she always seems to be the one leaning back in discussions. Restraining your impulse to fire back a sharp response, you slow down to catch up to what is happening inside and around you, while also including your evaluation of what could be happening in her.

You are tempted to treat her like a problem to solve (or crush), but she is a valuable player on the team, and you want to gain altitude before impulsively responding. Perhaps you recognize a kernel of truth in her offense: You name it as being hurried . . . or insensitive . . . or misreading her intent. You apologize, learning to use words that support your feelings, and begin to build a bridge of connection.

Perhaps you ask her how she'd like to be engaged in team discussions, and you hear more of her desire for collaboration. You start exploring for patterns and perspective around how this person became hurt. You are curious about how her needs are interacting with the team dynamic. You are moving from linear problem solving to complex leadership and ultimately to emotionally intelligent facilitation. This is progress indeed.

Connect. In time, leaders who actively practice the principles of Contact and Communicate will begin to learn how to Connect with people and the facets of life to become more collaboratively integrated. This joining of emotional forces and tapestry of healthy connection moves you toward internal and external unity.

When the collaborative Self is accessed, you are placing your problems and pains within the context of a greater, more widely informed whole. Connected leaders are those who are not only noticing themselves but starting to bridge their inner and outer worlds.

When you encounter an aggressive customer at work, notice how tight your chest is and then connect that tightness to feelings of fear and thoughts of failure. You catch yourself more quickly, realizing that this customer is simply a trigger, not the cause. And you name it, at least to yourself. With that clarity, you can then leverage this greater self-awareness to respond with more confidence and compassion. The customer feels heard despite not getting their way, and you feel empowered. You were triggered but not overrun. This is a momentous shift.

Commune. Very few leaders enter the realm of core Communion with themselves and others. Our westernized independence, the enticing climb up the corporate ladder, and the influence of the technological age are just some of the threats that keep leaders from experiencing the depth and intimacy of self in this life.

Many people make partial Contact, some learn to effectively Communicate, and a few appreciate the rewards of Connection, but the wholeness of Communion is elusive. A rare find indeed. It's not difficult to develop the core competencies and disciplines of business leadership; these require only foresight and perseverance. Deep transformation and the forging of lasting substance, well, that's more challenging.

Substance is a word that rings true in describing those entering the experience of Communion. It is one of my own personal convictions that communion with God is essential for communion with self and others. I believe we can only truly offer others what we have first received for ourselves. We love because we were first loved. We lead because we were once led. There is a substance of character, a gravitas, available for those willing to put in the work to become emotionally seasoned.

Do you want to be settled and centered at the core of your being? Communion offers us a worthy destination. While the marketplace inundates us with deadlines and deliverables, it's time to honor those realities while also transcending them to live intimately with ourselves and others. This is the essence of Communing.

When it comes to taking these four laps in Step 1, the age-old struggle with Self can be illuminated in one question: *Are you about the journey or the destination?*

Instinctively, I loathe the journey. The best thing about a ten-mile hike is the last three steps to my car after the exhausting expedition, knowing I've earned myself some steak tacos on the drive home. Road trip, no. Flying, yes. Novel, no. Executive summary, yes. Thankfully, I have a wife who loves the journey and our almost two decades of marriage confirms that about her.

Through my doctoral research in the field of deep change and transformation, it is glaringly obvious that you have to have an appreciation of and commitment to pathways of change. Or, in other words, the journey. There are those who market silver bullets and breath mints for instantaneous results, and while those pique my interest and may be helpful, they often only address the symptoms rather than the roots. We all want movement, but the steps we take must be part of a strategic process that delivers long-term sustainability.

When I am presenting my services to new clients, it's common to be asked if we can add more people, condense the work, and get done faster. Transactions are the name of the game in the world of commerce. But not in the field of transformative change. Transactions are part of the process, but only when they serve the greater context of systemic change. Not everyone thinks like this, which reinforces the *journey vs. destination* and the *profit vs. people* tensions I see so often in leaders.

Growing a Core Self is just that. Nurturing a journey that matures over time is like a fine wine. Hmm . . . Tuscany, wine, cheese, sunshine. *Sorry, what was I saying?* The journey from the head to the heart that meets our deepest desires for self and others is not a straight line. Nor is it a quick one, two, three leadership punch for instant health and well-being. The four Catch-Up points are an invitation to slow down and focus on data points that offer increasing self-awareness and potential growth.

I'll wrap this chapter with another great insight from Laloux: "The ultimate goal in life is not to be successful or loved, but to become the truest expression of ourselves, to live into authentic selfhood, to honor our birthright gifts and callings, and be of service to humanity and our world."[33] That's the big picture, and the Heart-Engaged EQ System is a simple, effective way to take that journey.

You've just survived the first step toward engaging your heart. Not too tough, right? And now it's time to take the next exciting step in this process. You're already growing and starting to engage a more authentic expression of yourself. Can you feel it?

CHAPTER 4

FINDING YOUR FEELINGS

*When we can talk about
our feelings, they become
less overwhelming, less
upsetting, and less scary.*
MR. ROGERS

A FEW MONTHS AGO, I was leading a one-on-one intensive with an executive, and I wanted to make a point about how hard it is to allow other people to have their own feelings when we haven't learned to hold our own feelings first. We were discussing the topic, but a principle is better learned through an experience than a speech so I thought I would try something.

I was going to share with this leader a vulnerable feeling I had experienced earlier in the day. But before I did anything, I got up from my chair, walked to the other side of the room, and wrote down one word on a piece of paper. This one word was my prediction of his immediate response after I shared my feeling. I'm not much into parlor tricks, but we had a great initial connection, and I thought it could be fun (if I was right) to show him how predictably people respond to the vulnerability of others.

I asked Max what he felt when arriving at the leadership intensive that morning having never met or talked to me before that moment.

"Well, I showed up eager to learn. I knew these two days would be an opportunity for growth, and I was excited. Yes, 'excited' is the word I would use."

"Gotcha. Do you want to know what I felt?" I asked Max.

"Yeah, tell me."

Locking eyes to strengthen the connection, I said, "When the doorbell rang this morning, I noticed that a part of me was afraid."

"Afraid? Really? Why?"

Then I smiled. "Go over to the table across the room and read the word I wrote down. That word was my prediction of how you would respond to my feelings disclosure. He walked over, took a look, and burst out laughing. "How did you know? Seriously how did you know that's what I was going to say?"

Written on the paper was the word *Why*.

Max was both impressed and curious. How could I have known that when I told him I was afraid, he would likely respond by asking why? Because this is utterly predictable.

When we offer someone our true feelings, it's common to be met with some version of, "What's that about? Explain yourself." The unfortunate reality of this response is that it puts the other person—someone who just took the risk of sharing something vulnerable—on the defensive. Now he or she has to subconsciously justify the feeling. There is a way to ask a curious *why*, but it has to be learned and delivered skillfully; typically, a *why* question to a confession of feelings becomes more transactional than invitational.

The experience had illuminated an important principle, and Max was grateful to become more aware. He asked me what he could say instead that would be more inviting to those who took emotional risks like I had. "Tell me more" is a good one. Notice the difference? "Tell me more" invites curiosity, about the person's feelings and experience, affirming that you are present and available—willing and desirous to enter another person's inner world.

The good news, as you are learning, is that you don't have to do anything about someone's feelings other than receive them. Feelings don't need fixing; instead, they need to be shared, preferably with those who can show up as a compassionate witness rather than a problem-solver. In this chapter, you're going to learn how to name your feelings and how to be present with the feelings of others in a healthy way.

This is Step 2 of the Heart-Engaged EQ System. After you connect to your body, notice your thoughts, refresh your meaning, and identify your feelings, it's time for a deeper dive into the feelings. *Just as you can't lead others effectively until you can lead yourself skillfully, you can't develop emotional intelligence with others until you enlarge your understanding of yourself.*[34]

Learning to Speak "Heart"

How do you feel? The question can be a strange one for many folks. It beckons us into places we don't fully understand— places that are often intimidating and insecure. And really, what's the point? It's not like we can change these pesky emotions anyway.

Feelings, much like the color of our blood, like death and desire, remind us that we are all equally human, created with common realities, common motivations, and common bonds that transcend the intricacies of our individual lives. We all have our stories of brokenness and brilliance that contain different characters, plot twists, and outcomes, yet we all identify with an extremely similar set of feelings, hopes, and emotional experiences. We're much more alike than different.

"How are you feeling?" It's a question we ask someone when we think he or she is not doing well. More common is, "How's it going?" It's an expression of casual interest, inviting an easy but surfacy liturgy in response. You can expect to hear a handful of socially accepted and conditioned responses. Give it a try. Ask a couple of people how they feel and note the number who respond with some variant of the following.

"Yeah, I'm fine. Thanks. Things are busy."

"I'm good. How 'bout you?"

"Excellent! Glad it's almost Friday."

Fine, good, and *excellent.* These habituated words keep things safe and familiar, adhering to the rules that support productivity. *The intent is to invite comfort rather than any real truth-telling.* Both parties engage in the mechanics of a caring conversation, and many do indeed care, but this approach limits the relational risks and rewards. Neither side expects any particular depth or meaning.

A person is more likely to ask, "How are you doing?" than "How are you feeling?" Even in casual banter, we have a subconscious preference for activity over emotion. If the response veers outside the lines of expected parameters, the person asking has a ready backup plan to cut vulnerability off at the pass. The social contracts we make in most spheres come with some pretty significant boundaries, and leaders are good at subtly reinforcing them.

A Heart-Engaged person is one who is learning to be more comfortable in his or her own feelings so that person can ask others about theirs, and then sticks around with tolerance, curiosity, and connection rather than immediately jumping ship. Ask anyone who knew me in my late teens and twenties, and you'll hear just how quickly I could escape a conversation headed toward any form of emotional intensity.

As Jack Nicholson and I wrote in *The Human Operating System*:

> The willingness to reflect upon our primal emotions and process them within relationships of trust allows greater awareness and confidence to take hold in the conscious mind. The empathy we receive from a trusted relationship is critical to working through our

resistance. This can be a mentor, a counselor, a wise friend, a trusted advisor, or a loving spouse, but the decisive step revolves around our vulnerability. The risk to move beyond fear with a safe companion propels us across this threshold and into the next stage.[35]

A Shared Language

My wife Natalie tells an amusing story about her father who was in Switzerland decades ago with her brother and some of their bandmates during a European music tour. Her dad was trying to get directions to their destination in a small mountain town high in the Alps, but since this was no metropolitan city, he was faced with a formidable language barrier. Impulsively, he burst into the only foreign language he could speak: Spanish. Needless to say, despite his best efforts, the attempt was in vain. The Swiss-German speakers simply looked at him blankly. There was no common language to bridge the connection gap.

Shared language is a vital tool for progress. Speaking and understanding the same words is the priority, but when that is not possible, we may resort to pictures, hand gestures, or interpreters. The end goal is always the same—to forge a connection so people can communicate and collaborate toward some type of good outcome.

Learning to share an emotional language is equally important. Keep in mind that even when the words are the same, there are still nuances and challenges to work through, including slang, dialects, and accents.

My early days in America came with some interesting challenges, particularly when talking to people on the phone. Despite speaking the same language, technically, my South African accent conspired to make words like water, bath, aluminum, howzit, and braai either undecipherable or unknowable to the receiver.

"Hi, I'd like to get my water connected at my new apartment, please."

"Your what?"

"My water. WATER. I need to get my water turned on."

"I'm sorry. Can you say that one more time?"

Gah, is this for real? I twist my tongue to squeeze out my best American accent, "My waaater. I need to switch on my waaater."

"Oh water, yeah sure. Sorry, I couldn't understand you."

Over time, I have learned to speak slower, articulate better, and at times choose another word entirely so I can bridge the gap and connect more deeply in my conversations. Feelings are very much the same. We need to establish the words, the definitions, and the rules of engagement for using a common emotional language.

In the last chapter, we introduced the idea of a "Core Self"—that part of ourselves that is most essential and fundamental to our being, beyond personality and behavior. Now I want to introduce the idea of "Core Emotions" as a set of feelings common to the human experience. It is important that we get extremely comfortable with these particular feelings so we can begin to name them in ourselves and find some dexterity in how we manage them internally and intra-personally. This is what I mean by a shared language and a common culture of emotional intelligence.

My friend Jeff Schulte first introduced the practice of Core Emotions to me using Chip Dodd's Eight Feelings. Looking down at a laminated sheet with those eight words, I began to say out loud the ones I could recognize within myself. It's a way of exercising the heart, and the more I practiced, the more I was able to notice. And the more I noticed, the more I became emotionally unblended. It felt clumsy at first, given my lack of emotional fluency, but in time, this practice impacted my life. It became both comforting and empowering to be able to call out what was happening in and around my life and explain how I was experiencing it.

Through practice and research, I discovered a whole gamut of primary-feeling sets from people like Darwin, Ekman, Plutchik, Pia Mellody, Susan David, Brené Brown, and countless others. To be clear for those who know and care, I am using the term Core Emotions from a socialized perspective more aligned with affect labeling and not Core Emotion Theory. I am a socially motivated leader who wants to help people gain a personal, cultural, and socialized resource—a shared language to better express the complexities of our "insides" together.

Historically, emotions have occupied the forefront in the psychology world, but less so in the leadership arena where mission, vision, values, operations, and process-improvement rule the roost. In the corporate space, feelings have long been held suspiciously at arm's length, and in some of our corporate gatherings, you can watch the expressions change as I introduce emotional language; you'd think I had thrown a six-foot rattlesnake into the room. But it doesn't take long to begin to normalize feelings as the most universal of all languages and a vital part of our shared humanity.

Over time (taking care not to prematurely sell what I had learned instead of sharing what I had embodied), I learned to educate and mentor corporate executives in the practice of Core Emotions and started groups focused directly on helping leaders become more emotionally engaged with their feelings in ways that invite movement toward their mission and connection with those they lead.

One of the best ways to become more emotionally resilient is to practice recognizing your feelings (Contact) and saying them out loud (Communicate) to trusted others who share the same desire and speak the same language (Connect). There is something magical about giving an external voice to our internal stirrings. Our mouths offer a physical confession in ways that bring courageous witness to the critics, judges, shamers, and punishers that rummage through our emotional systems. Learning to first access, then identify, and finally share your feelings is vital for the sustainability of those who desire to be truly human.

"Perhaps the easiest way to gain concepts is to learn new words," says neuroscientist Lisa Feldman Barrett. "You've probably never thought about learning words as a path to greater emotional health, but it follows directly from the neuroscience of construction."[36] Similarly, Marc Brackett says a child who lacks the permission and vocabulary to express and understand feelings will fail to learn how to manage complex emotions, leading to an array of personal and professional challenges.[37] We have little hope of understanding and managing the complexity of our emotional lives until we agree on a common language and are willing to start sharing more authentically with others about what is going on inside of us.

Leaders who want to deepen their EQ and strengthen their hearts will need to commit themselves to learn this language. For some who have consciously or subconsciously exiled their emotions, this language may be harder to appreciate. And on the flip side, even those who consider themselves emotionally expressive will have to do the work of forming their emotional core. Like anything, this work requires desire and dedication, so let's get started.

Learning the Big Twelve

Theories and hypotheses about emotions date back centuries. In fact, basic or primary emotions are referenced in the *Book of Rites*, a first-century Chinese encyclopedia.[38] Emotion is much harder to measure and properly define than many other human responses. But much of the study that has been done in emotional psychology is about basic emotions, our psychological and behavioral responses, and the role of emotional intelligence in our lives.

The twelve Core Feelings identified in this EQ model reflect an aggregate of the research on affect labeling, my personal experience, and alignment with the frameworks that Jack

Nicholson and I established around our *Human Operating System*. We reinforce leadership approaches that align with the systemic nature of human design: heart, soul, mind, and strength (body). These are our quadrants. This book is focused specifically on your heart quadrant so you can integrate the growth and development here back into the whole.

What you will notice with these twelve feelings is that there are six above the horizontal line and six below the line. The feelings above the line are going to be more socially constructed or supported (ashamed could likely fit those parameters, too, at times). They are more visible, external, and tangible. The feelings below the line are going to be the more tender, vulnerable feelings that are often more privatized and internalized.

AFRAID	**ANGRY**
CONFIDENT	EXCITED
LOST	**GUILTY**
SAD	**ASHAMED**
CALM	CARED-FOR
LONELY	**HURT**

Before we go any further, let's engage these feeling-words on a more personal level. Pause for a moment to center yourself. Take a deep, conscious breath or two. Connect to your body, notice your thoughts, refresh your meaning, and now look at the twelve feelings. Go ahead and say out loud which of these feelings are true for you right now. If you have a journal handy, you might want to write down your *now* words.

Just name your feelings instinctively before your more analytical frontal lobe gets in the way. We spend our lives in overdrive, trying to understand everything, but we have to learn to settle into the visceral experience of our moments, days, and seasons before trying to make sense of them. *What are you feeling?* You don't have to explain, defend, or justify your answers. It's enough to simply finish this sentence: "I feel . . ."

Are there some feelings missing from my list? Yes, of course. But remember, I have selected a set of Core Emotions to offer us a shared language of emotion, so think of them like building blocks or primary colors. Once we start to use the same words and subscribe to the same rules of engagement, our emotional intelligence takes on new energy and potential. If you want to add, take away, or use another set, go for it. I would suggest starting with these twelve for now.

For years now, I have been facilitating groups where six or eight leaders show up each week—in person or online—to look at a simple feeling sheet, to practice identifying their feelings, and to say them out loud so they know that have been heard. The qualitative and quantitative results have been astounding, both on personal and professional fronts.

Mike is one of our group participants. He was invited by a friend to join us and explore ways to start showing up to his insides. An engineer who had powered his way up the ladder, Mike had come to realize the toll it had taken on him, his wife, and their family. Saying yes to one thing always means saying no to something else. He had gained the world, so to speak, but was at risk of losing his soul.

"Rob, I don't think I know how to feel anymore. I am afraid that if I don't face this, it is going to cost me dearly."

The good news for Mike was that he did actually know how to feel. He had just told me he was afraid, and that's one of the twelve core emotions. I asked him what troubled him enough to reach out and call me.

"If I don't do something, I may lose my family."

"And then what?" I answered.

"Well, life would be hard."

I asked him what *hard* meant. I pressed him to go deeper. He had made contact and was attempting to communicate, but he had not yet reached connection. I wanted him to stretch a little further.

"Uh . . . *hard* means I would be left alone. My wife could leave me, and that would suck."

"Yeah, wow. That's super scary, and a real possibility."

I let the space deepen the moment. "What would it look like to move beyond holding your relationship together, and actually create a relationship worth living for? What if, instead of spending all that energy trying to keep someone from leaving you, you began to use that energy to build a more purposeful vision together? What kind of marriage would you fight for? What kind of marriage would make her want to stay and reinvest in your future?"

After joining one of my EQ Groups, Mike began to learn how to exercise his heart every week for an hour with seven other business leaders across the country over Zoom. Fear and self-preservation had prompted this step, yet within weeks, he was rediscovering his emotional core and building the momentum to keep showing up. Thankfully, Mike went on to recover both his heart and his marriage. The journey paid off.

Deep fears of abandonment drive many of us toward self-preserving and controlling behaviors. You may have been abandoned in big or small ways as a child, only to find that the effects carried into your adult life and leadership. Maybe you are hyper-vigilant at work and exhausted by overthinking. Maybe you are depressed from having to armor up and trying to dodge the possibility of new wounds. Maybe your life becomes one big, dismissive "whatever" with the people in your life.

A year later, Mike looked me fiercely in the eyes over lunch. "This feelings group may have saved my life. It definitely saved my marriage. I will never be the same because of it. Thank you. I know there will always be more work to do, but thank you."

I reminded him that the group is a powerful setting for this work because it provides a container for deep change. But safe containers aren't enough; it was his courage to show up week after week with the determination that catalyzed and reenforced the change. His commitment also challenged others to show up with more authenticity of their own. Like dozens of leaders in our groups, Mike learned how to access his heart in ways that have exponentially enlarged and enriched many different dimensions of his life.

On the following pages, I want to introduce each of the twelve Core Emotions in our rubric, along with the brilliant and broken sides of each. I call these variations "gold" and "shadow" and use this approach in much of my work to expand the scope of participants' awareness, understanding, and opportunity behind their feelings. As you come to understand these emotional themes, you will find deeply familiar yet startlingly new resources for your journey through life.

Afraid

Do you ever feel afraid? I hope so. I would hate to be the only one. Being afraid is a normal response to life on earth. Accessing the feeling of fear may even keep you alive in a dangerous situation! If you are not able to feel fear, you are probably living in denial or detachment. And if fear is a difficult emotion to access, it may come from an emotional background that taught you to dismiss feelings that suggest weakness.

There is truly much to be afraid of in this world. I read regularly about newly discovered threats that have the potential to injure or even kill us. And even if they don't kill us, we are all in the process of dying anyway. That's sobering. Life

BEING AFRAID
IS A NORMAL
RESPONSE TO LIFE
ON EARTH.

is extraordinarily beautiful but also profoundly scary. The most confident, resilient leaders are those who are aware of their fears and use that awareness to help them make better decisions.

I have noticed a concerning trend in the leadership sphere that promotes the message of being "fearless." My advice is to be cautious when you encounter books, conferences, or coaches that dismiss the feeling of being afraid. The absence or denial of fear diminishes our humanity and actually impoverishes our experience. Not to mention that the clinical absence of fear is the domain of psychopaths and sociopaths, which is not exactly the culture we want to encourage in our homes and workplaces.

Conversely, leaders, teams, and organizations that normalize fear and create comfortable dialog around it build a culture in which humans can work and thrive and develop courage and competence along the way.

Shadow. The dark side of fear is rooted in a fundamental *anxiety* and often leads us to over-compensate by trying to *control* people and situations. When we avoid our Core Emotions, we can expect to experience the pathology of the shadow sides as we attempt to suppress or manage a particular emotion. I mentioned some of the influence Chip Dodd has had on my understanding of Core Emotions and have appreciated how he links anxiety, control, and even rage to the darker side of being afraid.

Anxiety is a great medicator for our fears in that it distracts us from what we may actually fear so we don't have to face it. Dodd says, "Anxiety takes us away from what is true and makes us fretful, distrustful, impulsive, and controlling. In anxiety we rob ourselves of daily living and its experience. Instead, we try to control our future in order to prevent the recurrence of painful past experiences."[39]

Control is another effective but harmful distraction. If you feel afraid or are trying to protect yourself against fear, control offers an alternative. This is my personal addiction of choice, and I often feel like I'm in recovery. Whether your jam is control or anxiety, both are harmful in that they disconnect us from the root emotion we are facing.

Dodd illuminates the dynamic further. When the medicators of anxiety or control fail to contain the fear, some may go to rage. "Rage is a physiological experience that defends against vulnerability by disconnecting or denying true fear."[40] I think rage is powered by a volatile combination of fear and anger, depending on the situation. Regardless, we rage to squelch fear rather than process it or force our anger rather than turn to advocacy. You can rage silently, too, by the way. It doesn't have to be all kicking and screaming. The next time you find yourself raging, controlling, or anxious, hit the pause button and get curious: *What could I be afraid of? What is behind my raging anger?* You may discover the root of your troubles and get closer to the source.

Gold. But fear isn't all bad. Although we tend to avoid things that cause fear, our work invites people to engage with the twelve core feelings to harvest their particular gift. And the particular gifts that fear offers are *discernment* and *refuge*. The golden opportunity in feeling afraid is uncovering a genuine need and using the gifts of discernment and refuge to gain clarity and perspective around our fears and threats. When the danger is real, we can promptly and courageously find safe harbor somewhere or with someone to weather the storm. Perhaps there was an oversight at work, and you are deeply afraid it could cost you your job. You never meant to screw up, but you did. And now you fear the consequences. Fear is a deeply uncomfortable, even miserable reality. For the sake of self-preservation, you're tempted to defend, blame, hide, control, or medicate. But you also sense that there's another way, a new option.

Instead of defaulting immediately to panic, you pause long enough to catch up to yourself. You reach for that still center by taking a few deep breaths. You are able to name the emotion: You're afraid of the negative possibilities that could play out because of your oversight. Instead of letting the fear turn frantic, you begin to tap into your inner discernment, and if needed, reach for help and refuge.

Discernment is a powerful attribute for us to cultivate. Lisa Feldman Barrett says that, "The function most frequently associated with fear is the protection from threat."[41] In life, where almost anything can become a threat, this kind of perception is a valuable gift to help us live and lead with more awareness. Discernment becomes an internal risk-management system to process the realities of your fear and the possibilities of your need, based on your non-anxious perception.

To some degree, being afraid helps us prepare and deliver. Fear drives action, and often that action requires courage.

Using fear strategically helps us avoid panic responses and choose smart ones instead. Deadlines create anxiety that pulls us out of complacency to deliver outcomes. The expectations of others may create fear initially, but they also help us uncover the motivation to rise to meet them.

Robert M. Yerkes and John Dillingham Dodson were two Harvard psychologists who conducted a study demonstrating that moderate levels of anxiety could drive improved performance in humans and animals, but too much anxiety would flip the switch and drastically impair performance.[42]

On the other hand, if workplace deadlines and expectations are clearly unreasonable or indefinitely extended, if everything rises to the level of an emergency with your boss, then a healthy adaptation of the fear emotion calls you to engage that conversation with honesty.

Confident

Confidence feels fantastic, doesn't it? Confidence is a quality that's fueled by congruency between your external opportunities and your inner resources. From this place of alignment, confidence emerges to remind us, "You've got this! You are experienced, prepared, and competent."

Just don't get confidence mixed up with blind bravado or untested enthusiasm. Have you ever dropped into a half-pipe on a skateboard? I doubt many of you more "seasoned" leaders can relate but some of the younger ones may. As half the board hangs out over the edge—just waiting for you to lean on your front foot and head straight down the incline—you might wonder if your life insurance policy is up to date. Yet ten feet away, you'll see a sixteen-year-old making it look like a cakewalk. The difference between glory and disaster is often well-earned confidence.

The last thing my son Noah is thinking about when he is skating is the drop-in. He is well beyond that and instead wonders which tricks to perform on the other side of the ramp. He has full confidence he will make a textbook drop down the face of the ramp and come up the other side on his feet.

Think about the confidence that comes with losing weight during a ninety-day program. You stand a little taller, and the newfound confidence in your body translates into your posture and even your eyes. The dread is gone when it's time to take off your shirt and join the other dads at the neighborhood pool. Your hard work has paid off, and it feels good to be you again. Can there be a shadow side to an emotion that feels this good?

Shadow. The potential dark underbelly of confidence is the slide toward *arrogance or carelessness.*

"Nobody beats me at table tennis," I taunted my friends years ago.

Jason challenged my confidence by expressing his own. "You're only undefeated because you have never played me."

The challenge was made, and I responded with cocky boldness. "Let's go."

Jason was the CEO of a tech company in California and told me to meet him at his office the next day, and we could settle the matter in his corporate break room. I showed up to his huge building in my sandals, shorts, and t-shirt . . . because, you know, that's what young men wear in Southern California. After a key card, guest pass, and being chaperoned to his office, my earlier confidence was waning. *Why does he have a table tennis set in his office?* My concern was too late. Jason crushed me that day and brought my reign as table tennis champion to a screeching and humbling halt.

The stakes are low when arrogance is limited to good-natured competition, but that's not always the case when confidence runs amok. Unrestrained confidence often leads to carelessness with things that really matter. Just ask Bernie Madoff about the consequences of hubris when it comes to running a Ponzi scheme: 150 years in federal prison and $170 billion in restitution.

Gold. The golden side to confidence is *action and purpose.* The inner lift of a right-sized confidence empowers your reach for matters of deep meaning and significance—for defying artificial limitations and achieving greatness. When we feel confident, we feel strong, and when we feel strong, we want to do something about it. Without the vital quality of confidence, we find ourselves insecure, frozen, and second-guessing ourselves.

Have you ever written a challenging email and then hovered over the "Send" button, concerned your message might be met with resistance or aggression? Your confidence is being tested. You believe in what you have written and have taken the time to consider your words carefully, but then wonder whether you have the inner resolve to risk sending it. But as you take a lap of checking in with your body, mind, soul, and feelings, you find that inner core of belief. Yes, this is the right message, expressed in the right way and at the right time. You hit "Send" and your words blast through cyberspace. Confidence has released your voice and helped you take a stand for something that matters.

A less practiced, yet unbelievably strong expression of leadership confidence can be something on the other side of the equation: recognizing and sharing your lacks or inadequacies. Confident leaders are those who can name their incompetence without fear or shame. Rather than being threatened or driven to pretense, they boldly acknowledge their limits and catalyze the gifts of others to address challenges and bring home the win.

Lost

Do you remember driving to new places before smartphones? Back in the day, the well-prepared motorist always had a printed map book behind the driver's seat. As kids, we would page through it to occupy ourselves on long road trips. And even with the map, you still periodically got lost and had to stop and ask for directions. Not today. The rise of digital technology has made us more self-sufficient and independent. We now have personalized access to anyone, everyone, and anything (when cell coverage works) from the comfort of our own handheld magic box. Including GPS directions.

There were several tumultuous seasons in my early childhood which resulted in my older brother Richard and me being sent off to live with our grandparents for a while on a farm of several thousand acres called Glenfillan. Set in a remote part of South Africa, the farm still holds the residue of magical memories. Through some hard introspection in more recent years, I have come to realize how those formative experiences shaped me in both positive and negative ways that still play out in my life and leadership today. I can now see how complex those years were for all of us I have so much more perspective on how lost I felt. Not only was I literally above the clouds in those mountains, but I was a child trying to find a sense of my real home while living so far away from it.

Children growing up in households marked by dysfunction face a triple challenge. They are forced to reconcile feeling lost, lonely, and powerless all at the same time. Thankfully, children are also gifted with underdeveloped comprehension and remarkable resiliency. While they may be recording much of their early stories subconsciously, they don't quite have the tools to realize the severity and implications of their reality while it is happening.

But feeling lost is not just an experience for children. You have likely found yourself lost for a moment, a season, or even longer. "Lost" is a common human experience if you know how to see it and own it within your life. Surely you have shown up to work on a Monday morning on some obscure day in the middle of a cold winter and asked yourself, "What the hell am I doing with my life?" When leaders feel lost, they are being invited by this emotion to locate themselves within their story.

Being lost is not quite so scary or shameful for me anymore. The older I get, the more I realize life is damn complicated. If I don't feel lost once and while—in my job, my home, my friendships, or my purpose—I'm likely not venturing beyond the safe confines of my own limitations. It is hard to get lost if you never leave home. Part of pioneering, chasing, stretching, and growing is learning to reach into the great unknown and break new ground.

Shadow. The problem is not being lost. The problem is what happens if you don't recognize that you're lost. The shadow dimension of this emotion is becoming *vulnerable* and *defenseless*, fearing *desertion* when they call off the search party. Naked and afraid, you feel separated from the herd, and even from yourself. You may find yourself feeling anxious and frantic with no clear line of sight to navigate through. It is both scary to be lost and scary to lose someone. In Africa with all our fantastic wildlife, everyone knows that you are safest in the pack. Even an animal as fierce as a buffalo or as large as an elephant can become a potential meal if they lose their way in the jungle and get separated from the herd.

In the workplace or the home, there is nothing worse than a person who is lost but won't admit it. Have you ever been at the mercy of a CEO leading without a compass? Such leadership inflicts significant consequences on those in their wake. Have you ever been the passenger in a car to an overly aggressive spouse who is adamant they know where they are going when it's painfully obvious that they don't? Okay, maybe that's me. (Sorry, Natalie.)

While feeling lost is normal, failing to attend to your lostness can set you up for more dangerous outcomes. In the corporate space, the feeling of being lost is often best unspoken. So it's no surprise when leaders hide, pretend, or get more aggressive to compensate. But when leaders take the risk to admit they are lost, they also earn the right to transform this emotion into constructive energy, not only for themselves but also for their teams.

Gold. The golden opportunities for leaders who can accept, without fear or shame, the feeling of being lost is that they can turn this experience toward fresh *discovery*. New ideas and opportunities must first be unknown before they can be known, which means we must enter unfamiliar territory to find new treasures. Or sometimes, to be found.

Admitting we feel lost often invites others in our lives to draw closer and offer their perspectives and companionship. The hiker being rescued, an adult finding his or her way on the other side of a divorce, a leader rescuing a contract with a client that was all but lost. There is a renewed sense of vitality and appreciation for life after finding or being found.

I remember being beautifully and uncomfortably disrupted by our first two babies early on in marriage. The feeling of lostness over several years was exceedingly real for both of us until one day, while alone together on a Caribbean cruise, Natalie and I looked up and saw each other again. *Oh, there you are! Where have you been? And where was I?* We found each other, and it was a memorable gift.

NEW IDEAS AND OPPORTUNITIES
MUST FIRST BE UNKNOWN
BEFORE THEY CAN BE KNOWN,
WHICH MEANS WE MUST ENTER
UNFAMILIAR TERRITORY IN
ORDER TO FIND NEW TREASURES.

While many people tell me how much they wish they had a mentor, few are willing to take any significant steps to search for one or enter the internal space that allows for such a relationship. To be mentored means to surrender your independence enough for another person to guide you to places you've never been. It means to be essentially lost and to welcome the opportunity to be led with humility.

Gratitude is the other golden gift of being lost. The experience of finding or being found usually elicits an instinctive response of thanksgiving. Maybe relief at first, but with deep gratitude in hot pursuit. And the posture of gratitude is one of the most transformative invitations of life. Receiving help and giving thanks positions us for optimism, resiliency, and breakthrough—absolutely essential qualities for a meaningful life and trustworthy leadership.

How do you feel so far? You've just covered the three Core Emotions from the "Mind of Heart" quadrant: afraid, confident, and lost. These three feelings correlate to the needs of the mind even though they enter our awareness through the heart. Have you felt any of these in the last twenty-four hours?

We're going to take two more chapters to unpack the experience of the rest of these Core Emotions so we all understand what we mean when we use the words. Even though the ideas contained in these twelve words are familiar, I want to describe what drives each feeling and how we experience both the dysfunctional shadowed side as well as the elevating golden side of each.

CHAPTER 5

FACING YOUR FEELINGS

*Be who you are and say what
you feel, because those who
mind don't matter and those
who matter don't mind.*

DR. SEUSS

I WAS TALKING WITH MY FRIEND RYAN recently about his experience in the world of feelings and leadership, and these are some thoughts from his journey.

"My grandfather was one of the most formative influences on my life as a child, and he knew how to show his emotions easily. He was free to be happy and free to cry, and he and my grandmother created a healthy and safe environment for me. My brother and I would be in and out of their house every week.

My mom, on the other hand, was actually bipolar. She would periodically go off the deep end. My dad left when I was nine, but my memory of him is that he *never* really showed his feelings. So I had the whole gamut of emotional expression modeled for me as a kid.

My mom's emotional outbursts stirred up a lot of shame and sadness for me. I knew something was wrong, but no one talked about it. I felt embarrassed, particularly at church. We ran in this upper-middle-class circle that my grandfather had created for us, and we were the odd duck. My mom particularly. People at church would just shake their heads and say they were praying for us. You know, that sort of 'bless your heart' southern thing. Kind of felt like pity.

So I worked hard to not be like my mom, to stuff my emotions like a lot of guys do and not show weakness. Emotions were not to be trusted; I think that was the overarching message of my childhood. Don't trust your emotions, and don't show weakness.

I also realized I had a temper, and once I get angry, I can get out of control pretty fast. That's been a theme throughout my life that makes me uncomfortable and contributes to my not wanting to acknowledge my feelings. They feel dangerous. Instead, I've tried to tamp that down, cover it up, and just climb the corporate ladder.

You know John McEnroe, right? Arguably the best tennis player of all time. Most people despised him, but I think he's awesome. When he channeled his anger, he could beat anybody. But when he let it get away from him, that's when he would do all the outbursts that people love to talk about. But I kind of identified with him because I was very angry. I also tried to channel that anger into doing stuff that would propel my career forward."

Ryan is not alone, of course. Many of us came, in various ways, to distrust our emotions, particularly the ones that felt vulnerable. As a result, our emotions became outcasts and rejects, orphaned parts of us that we would not own. But those pesky emotions don't actually leave; they simply go underground and then cause problems.

A big part of my work is not only reintroducing leaders to their castoff feelings but then trying to dial down the fear factor so we can both talk about them and face them in a safe way. Only then can we invite those prodigal emotions back home and reintegrate them into our psyche in a healthy way. We can own them and let them be part of us again in ways that strengthen relationships, not undermine them.

Just as we did in the last chapter, let's pause briefly and re-center. Take a couple of deep, conscious breaths. Check in with your body and notice sensations. Check in with your mind and notice your thoughts. Check in with your soul and refresh your meaning . . . and finally, take a fresh look at the twelve feelings, naming those that are present for you right now. *How does this help my leadership?* you may be wondering. For now, I ask you to keep trusting. We will soon unpack the incredible outcomes and deliverables that flow out of this work. Hang tight.

Now that you are building rapport with these different facets of your heart, let's continue to explore the next two heart quadrants: "Strength of Heart" and "Heart of Heart."

Angry

We naturally and normally feel angry when someone or something is not as it should be. Including yourself. When the world is not working the way I want, need, or believe it should, anger is the feeling that usually surfaces the loudest. We usually think of anger as a negative emotion, but it can be both negative and positive.

For example, I am angry about the host of injustices in our world. How can children be dying of starvation? How can biological parents abandon their own children? How can airborne sicknesses instantly appear, spreading like wildfire across the globe, leaving countless people to die alone? How can we live in a world where the lesser spotted pygmy frog gets more press and attention from city leaders than the women being human trafficked in that same town? I am so angry about these kinds of injustices. And at the same time, I often feel powerless to change them, which prompts me to ditch my anger and replace it with *indifference*. When that happens, I abandon the opportunity to turn my conviction into advocacy and fail to become an agent of change.

Anger is a loud social emotion, which is why it lives in the *strength of heart* quadrant. Being angry is way more appealing and easier to express than hurt or loneliness. I call this the "easy emotion." Notice the next time you are angry, *What else are you feeling?* Sometimes anger is a diversion from what's really going on inside.

The American Psychological Association reminds us that "anger is a completely normal, usually healthy, human emotion.

But when it gets out of control and turns destructive, it can lead to problems—problems at work, in your personal relationships, and in the overall quality of your life. And it can make you feel as though you're at the mercy of an unpredictable and powerful emotion."[43] This is why calling out the feeling of anger can be extremely calming. Anger needs to have some form of an audience, even if the audience is just you.

Shadow. We have an intuitive awareness of the shadow side of Anger, which accounts for our often-ambivalent relationship with this emotion. We are drawn to the power it contains and gravitate toward it under stress, but at the same time, we recognize that its dark side can easily turn destructive through *aggression* and *force*.

Marie shares some of her journey with anger:

> I always thought my dad was just an angry man, best to manage or avoid. I was so determined to not be angry like him growing up, so when my own anger welled up, I would swallow it. If I voiced my anger, I risked becoming agitated and aggressive like him. So I learned to make peace at any cost, which meant suppressing my own voice, needs, wants, and desires. I was praised for this in my family system (especially by him), but little did they know that it came at the cost of my own personhood.
>
> What I came to learn as an adult was that my dad's outbursts of aggression and rage were a convoluted blend of mismanaged anger combined

with fear, shame, and guilt. He was a scared man
trying his best to control an uncontrollable life,
and that toxic cocktail of emotion would come
out sideways. We children became the unfortunate
casualties of war between him and my mother.

And as we described earlier, the other shadow of anger
is *apathy* and *indifference*. Those who relinquish or dismiss
their legitimate voice of anger in a relationship simultaneously lose part of their essential personhood. And that cost
is too high. Indifference leads to distraction with less vital
things and eventually paralysis around the more vital things.
An apathetic expression of anger manifests as "Whatever" or
"Who cares?" and over time, calcifies.

Gold. "Anger is related to the *fight, flight, or freeze* response
of the sympathetic nervous system; it prepares humans
to fight. But fighting doesn't necessarily mean throwing
punches. It might motivate communities to combat injustice
by changing laws or enforcing new norms."[44] *What are you
angry about?* The feeling of anger reminds us that something
is wrong and must be fixed or at least tended to.

Anger invites the golden gift of *advocacy* and when we
get angry enough, we take our message to the streets with
necessary *action*! Advocacy is a passionate declaration of what
could be or what should be, usually on behalf of a weaker, less
powerful population. If you look behind the curtain at many
nonprofits, you often see an army of advocates who have given
their lives to fight for the things that make them fiercely angry.

AN ADVOCATE WHO IS
BOTH ANGRY AND HEALTHY
STANDS TRUE TO A
CAUSE . . . BUT ASKS
FOR TOLERANCE, NOT
TOTALITARIANISM.
FOR REDEMPTION, NOT
RETRIBUTION.

Over time, the mature expression of anger can overturn injustice and make a hugely positive difference in the world. The life and leadership of Nelson Mandela offers some powerful examples of both healthy and shadowed anger. The immature expressions of this feeling can slide quickly to the shadow side, so this can be a thin line for leaders to navigate.

Advocacy is beautiful when fueled by inspiration and invitation but can be off-putting when forced and demanded. An advocate who is both angry and healthy stands true to a cause or position but asks for tolerance, not totalitarianism—redemption, not retribution. Maturity allows space for different convictions and mutual respect, even when two opposing belief systems converge. Not all feelings of anger will drive you toward action and advocacy. Sometimes, anger just needs to be recognized, validated, and expressed so you feel heard (whether or not you get your way), and then you can move on.

Healthy anger is a great emotion to cultivate for those seeking to build an organization. You may be angry about how people are treated in your workplace, and that anger offers you a choice between apathy and advocacy. If you choose the latter, you find yourself becoming part of the solution. Your time, energy, efforts, and voice become dedicated to the cause of transforming the culture so your company can become a place where people are valued.

I have a healthy anger about the emotional health of leaders that stems from my need for more connection with myself and those I love. This book is a testament to the advocacy I have unlocked as a result of this anger. One does not simply read, research, and write a book about a topic you casually care about. I am motivated for you to recover more of your heart so you can offer more of your true gift to others. Anger drives my motivation.

If you noticed, Confidence also shares Action as a golden attribute, but it's the order that's different. With confidence, you move into action and that action then extends into mission, whereas the emotion of anger starts with a voice of purpose and then extends itself into action as the result. Subtle but different. Simply said, Anger and Confidence are two feelings that work together in powerful ways to help us feel, reach, and act.

Excited

When I was a kid, going to bed on Christmas Eve was the most exciting and torturous experience imaginable. Having weighed and shaken each wrapped gift under the tree, I was finally one sleep cycle away from finding out what was actually in them. Excitement and anticipation would course through my veins.

Is Christmas about Santa Clause or Jesus? As a child in many homes, the family intent was somewhat clear that Jesus was important, but the gifts under the tree stacked the deck in favor of Santa.

The feeling of excitement is just that—an exciting feeling. It's like a turbo boost. You only get so many of these moments, so when they come, it feels like electricity coursing through your veins.

We surprised our daughter Ella with tickets to a Taylor Swift concert for her tenth birthday. My wife created a treasure hunt that led her by clues and candles from the front door throughout the house to where she would discover a new outfit . . . and finally an envelope that contained the tickets.

Ella was beyond excited, and the suspenseful treasure hunt only elevated the payoff. She screamed for joy like a ten-year-old girl (literally) and grabbed both her mother and me to thank us over and over for the exciting experience that lay ahead. A few weeks later, she donned her new outfit, and my wife whisked her off to the show. She ended up getting a hug from Taylor's mom somehow, which only drove the experience to new heights. Her excitement and gratitude were contagious and deeply rewarding for us as well. What an emotion, this one, but even here there is a shadow side.

Shadow. The shadow of excitement is *sensationalism*, and with enough sensationalism in your life, you eventually have to resort to some level of *deception*, whether that be subconsciously deceiving yourself or others.

Have you ever been hyped up to meet someone important in your industry at a business event, only to have your excitement tip over into sensational idealism? You try to play it cool and act genuine but instead find yourself name-dropping and over-compensating to try to create a memorable impression. In truth, you have projected your ideal self, lathered in sensational breadcrumbs, at the cost of your Core Self.

And that's not all. Letting yourself feel excited sets you up for the potential risk of being let down. Dashed hopes leave us wanting to temper this feeling to minimize the possibility of pain. And not just random pain, but pain right at the point of an anticipated good. It's no wonder we might want to force the outcome rather than embrace this dangerous feeling and let the chips fall where they may.

Sensationalism promises to hedge against the disappointment of dashed excitement, but it cannot deliver. The *Oxford Lexicon* says sensationalism is "the presentation of stories in a way that is intended to provoke public interest or excitement, at the expense of accuracy.[45] Forcing or projecting excitement becomes the shadowed expression whether you are truly excited or not. The illusion of excitement can delay a hard reality by keeping the idea of excitement on life support.

Some version of this plotline peppers many movies: A young teenager is told his absent father is finally showing up to take him to a theme park for the day. He's thrilled! 9:00 a.m. gives way to 9:05 a.m. Then it's 9:30. *There must be traffic*, he mutters to himself bolstering hope. Finally, the hammer drops when the phone rings. "Sorry son," Dad says. "It's not going to work out today. Something came up. But next time, next time, okay?"

The despondency is palpable. The young man runs upstairs, devastated by the lost opportunity for fun, even more devastated by the lost intimacy and love. Something else matters more to his dad than he does. After a few rounds of this routine, the boy learns to squelch the possibility of excitement entirely. Why would you set yourself up for that? And sadly, another human succumbs to the harsh reality of a painful world they cannot change.

The boy desperately searches to replace this loss with

something more wildly imaginative; he accesses his inner sensationalist to push up and out to "better" things. Self-indulgence. Fixations. Addictions. He chases and forces counterfeit excitement. The feeling becomes sensualized and surreal. Rather than cherish the genuine moments of excitement when they arise naturally, he tries to capture them and demand more.

There is a new category of predator that has emerged in recent years—the social media influencer. They fake and spin counterfeit excitement to monetize their fan base. There are even studios you can rent to pretend you are in a private jet so your photos will project grandeur to an unknowing audience. Excitement sells, even if it's fake, and it's easy to pander to the temptation in our own lives and leadership.

Gold. The golden opportunity of excitement is *an infectious joy and energy*. Ever been in the bustling crowd of a professional athletic contest? Personally, I'm not much of a sports fanatic, but I have clients in some of the major leagues, so I end up at various games to enjoy them in my own way. Regardless of your investment in the sport, when your team scores, you feel the wave of excitement surge through the stadium. It's infectious. Your spirit can't help but rise to meet the energy. When others experience the excitement of a win, it provokes our own dreams of winning, whatever they may be.

Unfortunately, the hyper-individualized mindset in our western world hinders collaborative celebration and excludes the loser. There is always a losing team. Competition in sports is one thing, but in the world of commerce, that same attitude can kill a culture. The Heart-Engaged leader notices this tension and leans toward others who are excited and celebrates them, multiplying the energy of their win. Fan the flame. Notice it, express it, and watch the world become a more beautiful place for a moment in time.

I love being around people who are excited. The worst is being around someone who should be excited but isn't. Achievements roll in only to be trampled in a detached sprint for the next mountain to climb. Many face a dehumanizing work culture that withholds excitement, leaving its people in perpetual wonder if anything is awesome anymore. Learning to embrace excitement and give voice to it may be the very thing that solves your retention issues. Nobody wants to be around slave drivers and downers, and nobody wants to work for sensationalists who hype you up with empty promises.

Guilty

Feeling guilty sucks. There is no clearer way to say it. Nobody wants to feel guilty, but we all experience it. I don't like it one bit, but I am starting to experience the benefits of this emotion and am warming to it... wait am I? The sooner you start to accept the reality that guilt is a legitimate and necessary human emotion, the sooner you can harness the power of its purpose.

The feeling of guilt comes to me in many shapes, forms, and sizes. Its most common expression is when I have done something I know is wrong, or someone points out my wrongdoing. Or it can be the opposite: I feel guilty for *not* doing something I should have.

An old lady struggles to cross the road, and I blindly turn away. The invitation to donate to a charity presents itself, yet I impulsively snub the opportunity without any diligent consideration. My inaction can make me feel guilty in these moments. We may also experience the feeling of guilt, based simply on our thoughts, fantasies, and hidden desires, even if we don't act on them. You smile, say hello, and play along, yet hide your disgust. Have you ever wanted someone to pay because they have hurt you in some way? Guilty as charged. Something deep inside of you says this is wrong.

Guilt can be complicated though. What may be wrong and conjure up guilt in one culture or belief system may not in another. "Socially constructed" is the term used by Karen Caplovitz Barrett.[46] For example, in many states today, you could be arrested, prosecuted, and declared guilty for buying or smoking marijuana, while no such crime exists just one state line away. Did you know it is illegal to be reincarnated in China without government permission? You would be guilty of a crime if you do.[47]

The feeling of guilt can be instigated by external conditions or internal convictions. Postmodernity has only added more complexity to the topic, given that this worldview pushes for the relativity of truth. My personal faith holds that there is an absolute truth infused into all people everywhere that offers a sense of righteousness—a higher standard of which we are consciously or unconsciously aware.

Resting on top of that foundation are the ever-changing modifications, interpretations, or outright replacements that cultures and countries declare and enforce. In a world of relativity, I am thankful for the universal conviction that still believes people can be held liable for things like murder, child abuse, theft, slavery, or trafficking.

Shadow. "Well, sure I did it, but you need to know that you made me do it!" Look out for the word "but" when someone is offering an apology; chances are that it's a defense more than an admission of guilt. They have done something wrong but are failing to own it. When I feel guilt, I instinctively look for a way to justify my behaviors somehow. I may blame the system, the other person, or the circumstance.

Alternately, I go to self-deprecation. "I'm such a loser. I can never do anything right." I believe everyone in the world is guilty of something every day of their lives. Guilt is simply part of the human condition whether you like it or not. When *blame* and *shame* emerge as the shadow of guilt, you may feel like an utter disgrace to yourself and believe you deserve *punishment* in an attempt to atone for your wrongdoing or reset the scales of your guilty actions.

Before we turn to the golden side of guilt, let's draw one quick distinction between guilt and shame—an emotion that will have its own category next. While guilt says I *did* something wrong, shame says I am wrong.

In her book *Shame and Guilt in Neurosis*, Helen Block Lewis says, "The experience of shame is directly about the *self*, which is the focus of evaluation. In guilt, the self is not the central object of negative evaluation, but rather the *thing* done or undone is the focus. In guilt, the self is negatively evaluated in connection with something but is not itself the focus of the experience."[48]

Gold. The redemptive side to guilt offers us *forgiveness* and *freedom*. When we have done something wrong and feel guilty, we aren't stuck there. We have the ability to reach and ask for forgiveness in the hope of experiencing freedom. What an amazing opportunity and an equally amazing experience.

Do you remember the the last time you felt conviction that you injured someone, acknowledged your mistake, and asked for forgiveness? And then received it? It's an extraordinary feeling—a holy gift that one human can offer another. There is perhaps no greater contact with the divine than tasting the grace of forgiveness.

Of course, sometimes our conscience is activated, we realize we need forgiveness and ask for it, but don't receive it. For many reasons, people can withhold forgiveness, even though it hurts them and us. This doesn't mean we stay locked in the prison of someone else's judgment. We can always choose freedom—and forgiveness always leads to freedom. It's a lot easier when forgiveness is freely offered, but even when it's not, it can be freely received.

Can you feel the contrast between punishment and shame (the shadow side) and forgiveness and freedom (the golden side)? Both are powerful, yet one leads to a restoration of life and community while the other leads to judgment and alienation.

False Guilt. There is another form of guilt that emerges within my EQ groups from time to time. It begins with the naming of guilt as an emotion, yet upon deeper review, you realize it's not necessarily guilt at all. In this scenario, you have done nothing wrong, and the other person involved would agree, but you still feel like you have. You feel vaguely responsible and liable in some way. Sometimes this goes under the label of survivor's guilt.

I consider false guilt to be a blend of empathy, shame, and powerlessness. False guilt offers a sense of empowerment or the illusion that you must take responsibility for a wrong and make it right, even if it is not yours to begin with. You may feel guilty that your spouse is home alone during work hours feeling lonely, but perhaps the more accurate feeling would be sad. Is it really your fault? Likely not.

Is the loneliness real? Yes. But false guilt makes someone else's circumstances your responsibility and propels you to "fix" the situation. What if, instead, you could let the other person be responsible for identifying and sharing those feelings, and then take responsibility for simply being fully present in the sharing?

Perhaps instead of assuming false guilt, you respond with, "Thanks for sharing. Tell me more?" And eventually, you could ask, "Do you want or need anything from me to help you take action for change while I am at work?" False guilt is a diversion from the authentic offering that true guilt extends.

Now let's transition from the Strength-based emotions to

the most directly Heart-based of emotions: feeling ashamed, cared-for, and hurt.

Ashamed

Brené Brown is a brilliant researcher and presenter on the topic of shame. She has gone to great academic lengths to contextualize her research in ways that ordinary people can relate to. In her book, *Daring Greatly: How the Courage to Be Vulnerable Transforms the Way We Live, Love, Parent, and Lead*, Brown writes, "Shame derives its power from being unspeakable. That's why it loves perfectionists—it's so easy to keep us quiet. If we cultivate enough awareness about shame to name it and speak to it, we've basically cut it off at the knees. Shame hates having words wrapped around it. If we speak shame, it begins to wither. Just the way exposure to light was deadly to the gremlins, language and story bring light to shame and destroy it."[49]

Feeling ashamed is the "not enough" feeling. Brown and others challenge leaders to bring their limitations into the light so they can consider them honestly rather than be ruled and mocked by them. "Ashamed people frequently wish to get up and run out of the room, which they sometimes do. At other times they simply look down, avoid eye contact, and lower their shoulders seeming to shrink in size."[50]

Nobody likes to feel like they are not enough because this opens us up to any number of scary outcomes in a world that demands more than we can deliver. Not having what it takes to make it in your industry could mean losing a job, and losing a job means having to fumble through an uncertain future with a damaged sense of self-worth and undermined confidence. Feeling ashamed makes us want to hide lest we have our nose forced into our failures.

Despite the fact that shame can be utterly destructive, don't rule it out entirely. Shame can also be a productive emotion for many leaders. Fear and shame can both drive you in ways that other emotions cannot, which we'll explore in the Gold section.

Shadow. I never knew my biological father until later in life. I only saw him perhaps a half dozen times by the time I was thirty. What became evident to me was how trapped he has been his whole life by toxic shame and self-contempt. There are decisions he has never recovered from, and this defining experience has cost him any meaningful relationship with me or my children.

The work for me has been to grieve the loss while not allowing his abandonment to undermine my own value. There are only two human beings who can create you, and when one or both fail to move toward you, it's a significant obstacle to push through.

The liberating truth I have come to embrace is that it's not the job of children to make their parents love and pursue them. I spent many years longing, hoping, waiting, trying, helping, and over-functioning, but it is nearly impossible for a child to rescue a parent from shame's prison. I used to tell people how much my biological father missed out on my life. It took a friend, Jeff, to reverse the statement one day: "Rob, you missed out." It was easier to talk about how much my father has missed because of his shame but more sobering to own the loss and sorrow I have carried through this life fatherless.

Jeff coached me on a principle in our field of work: In traumatic situations, children often assume they are the problem to mitigate against feeling helpless within the choices of others. Making yourself the problem, even when you are not, offers a semblance of power rather than accepting the painful truth of your vulnerability.

Are there relationships in your life that are being hindered because your shame has gone toxic? Has your self-contempt or even your self-disgust gotten in the way of loving, leading, and living?

If the feeling of shame has its way with you, it can lock you into the belief that you are fundamentally broken and unworthy—that you are undeserving of love or goodness. It is healthy to accept the truth that we are limited and imperfect, which offers the possibility, but not the necessity, of shame. But this needs to be balanced with the reality that we are also remarkable, resilient, and gifted. If you over-inflate the value side, you edge over into unhealthy pride. Shame tempts us with the very real threat of *self-contempt* . . . and eventually *escapism* becomes a twisted act of retreat attempting to distract or distance ourselves from the feelings.

When we can no longer metabolize the feeling of shame, it's easy to try to numb its debilitating voice by over-indulging or self-medicating. These escaping strategies are short-lived at best, and at worst can dismantle all that is most precious to us. So it's imperative that we learn to navigate toward the gold of shame.

Gold. What possible gold could come from the feeling of shame? There is an acceptance of our limitations that can be both liberating and empowering. If shame says you are not enough, there can be a healthy acceptance that invites the gift of *humanness*. As humans, we seem to fall, fail, and fret ourselves forward in life. The acceptance of these limitations invites a healthy acceptance of our humanity and interdependence on others. We begin to learn how to reach, how to need, and how to draw on the resources of others and be better together.

Our fourth child was just a couple of months old when Natalie and I sat on the bed and had the most vulnerable conversation of our lives. With tears in her eyes, Natalie said, "Rob, I need more from you. I am juggling so much right now and need you to show up in several areas," and she went on to name them. She took the risk of sharing how I could do more and be more.

I listened and then responded soberly. "I hear you, and I love you, babe. But I am literally at my max right now. I simply don't have that to give."

She sighed and responded with a grieved, "I know."

From the honesty of that space, I responded with my own reach. "I, too, need more from you than what I am getting."

"I hear you. I wish I could do that, but I also don't have that to give right now."

Here we were, two individuals alone in our room, asking for more from the other. And both hearing an honest "no."

There was a feeling of shame that washed over both of us for not being able to power through our mess and be enough for each other. We could barely be enough for ourselves, never mind extending ourselves through trauma to be what the other person needed.

But rather than be crippled by the shadows of our shame, the next comment I made went for the gold. "Looks like neither of us is getting enough of what we need. *Do you want to be not enough together?*" We reached for each other, we wept, and we lay there on the bed until the tears subsided. Our marriage had crossed into a new depth of intimacy, and we knew that despite our unmet needs, we weren't going anywhere. We were in this for the long haul. We had both been broken down to the lowest common denominator, and in that humble place, we both said yes to "us."

Flash forward almost a decade later. A few months after my stroke, Natalie and I were in the closet talking. It began as a practical conversation and erupted into big emotions, reflecting the pressure cooker of health, trauma, and stress we were trying to survive. I managed to express the story that had been plaguing me like an open wound.

"My greatest fear right now is that I don't have what it takes. That in my weakness, I am not enough for you."

Natalie looked at me compassionately but didn't reassure me. She answered with as much kindness as she could. "I see your fear and shame, and I don't know how to say this, Rob, but it's true. Right now, you are not enough for me." She continued. "And my biggest fear is that I am too much

WE ARE FALLIBLE;
WE ARE LIMITED.
AND WHEN WE LEARN
TO ACCEPT THAT TRUTH,
IT HELPS US BECOME
MORE ACCEPTING OF FAILURE,
OURS AND OTHERS,
AS A NECESSARY TOOL
FOR LEARNING.

for you—that you are overwhelmed by me and my needs, by who I am right now."

"That's true," I replied. "You are too much for me. I feel overwhelmed, and don't know how to be with you right now."

This was a new kind of vulnerability. Our worst fears had been expressed in a dark closet, only to be confirmed. At that moment, we chose once again to say yes to each other. No conditions were set to make things different. Instead, we held each other with commitment and acknowledged the limitations of our humanity. Shame led to humility, which led to vulnerability, which led to greater intimacy.

At some point, a leader must accept that he or she is not enough and that he or she needs *help*. This humble admission allows that person to reach for others, for deeper insight, and for creative ways to push through. We are not superhumans. Even the most incredible people are not incredible at everything. We are fallible; we are limited. And when we learn to accept that truth, it helps us become more accepting of failure—ours and others—as a necessary tool for learning. Failure becomes an avenue, not an obstacle, to growth. In this way, the golden side of shame can actually drive you to reach for the people and resources you need to succeed.

Cared For

Feeling cared for sounds simple enough, but for many leaders I work with, this can be an extremely challenging feeling to access with any level of sincerity or depth. The insinuation is that children and old people need someone to care for them because they are weak, vulnerable, incompetent, or frail. I have spent my whole life striving to be strong, capable, and independent, so why would I be interested in the idea of someone caring for me? Well, for starters, without care, most everything will die or atrophy. I know I long for it, need it, and want it. Yet I resist it. This subconscious belief undergirds much of corporate culture and destructively impacts both the organization and the individual.

Do you care about your wedding ring, your new car, your vacation, or your pet? It's usually easy to answer these kinds of questions. The care you give these objects comes from the value you ascribe to them. Well then, *do you value yourself?* Do you value the other significant people in your life? The feeling of being cared for registers in your head and your heart as being deeply valued.

In a world of a bajillion people, this is beautiful. You are the starfish in the story, where another human has pulled you from the crowd and made deliberate choices to directly consider, value, and prioritize you. The goal is to be cared about for simply being ourselves and not just what we do for others. But either way, feeling cared for feels good. Will the feeling last? Not always. Few emotions are permanent, but slap on that cared-for aftershave and breathe in the rich aroma.

I believe this feeling is instilled in those who have been nurtured well in their early years. I often hear from leaders about how they were raised by parents who taught them to achieve, but few whose backstories suggest they were nurtured. The concept of caring for *others* comes more easily, right? But to be the recipient of care can be a foreign experience at best.

"Hey Joe, I'd love to grab a coffee and check in with you about how things are going. I know a lot has happened on the home front the last few months, and I care about you a lot."

"Sure thing," Joe replies, but he instantly feels defensive. *Why would my boss want to meet? What is this about? Is this the beginning of the end, or a warning that my fourth-quarter targets are approaching?* Nobody else on his team cares about how he's doing, so why would his boss be different?

Like many, Joe is suspicious when it comes to receiving the love, care, or attention of others. And there are valid reasons why people should be on their guard, especially in the marketplace. Hunkering down to avoid the vulnerability of being cared for may keep you safe, but only at the cost of keeping everyone out.

Shadow. The shadowed side of this feeling is *codependency* and *powerlessness*. When people are cared for without relational boundaries, they can be robbed of their own autonomy and can often stop taking responsibility for their own welfare. Need becomes expectation, which becomes presumption, and eventually, relationships and teams can become a melting pot of emotional quid pro quo. Caring for people is intrinsically good, except when it undermines sustainable self-care or facilitates dysfunctional behavior.

What's at stake in a codependent relationship is the proper interdependence and responsibility of relational power. When someone over cares, he or she is exerting power, and even if that exertion is well-intended, it requires the one being cared for to relinquish his or her own autonomy, power, and responsibility. This is appropriate in an emergency when someone legitimately needs rescuing. But as a long-term pattern, it locks the one being cared for in victimhood and powerlessness. A professional relationship could risk mimicking a parent-child dynamic and all boundaries go out the window for both parties.

Enabling can be the other effect of this shadowed emotion. When caring for people robs them of the consequences of their bad behavior, the natural corrective is removed and readily leads to situations that cause injury to themselves and others.

My friend Martin struggles with the practicalities of care. He is probably one of the most caring people I know but paired with a lack of boundaries, he can feel conflicted. Some leaders think that caring automatically means saying yes. But that's not necessarily true nor healthy. Sometimes the most caring thing you can do for someone is to say no because you have already said yes to someone or something else. Trying to play both sides usually ends in disappointment. Martin is doing the work to recover from a family rule his parents drilled into him growing up: that he should always be selfless in the service of others. He is learning now how to care for himself for the first time, and in doing so, finding more joy, purity, and priority in his motives to care for others.

Gold. The golden side of feeling cared for is *belonging*. We are all desperate to feel safe and secure within a tribe. When an employer truly cares about you (and not just your deliverables), you naturally lean in. There are times when we go through hard seasons and may need extra affirmation and attention, and in those times, opening yourself up to be cared for can be an incredible gift for both parties.

Caring for people communicates that they are seen, they are valued, and they are considered. To be wanted is the golden ticket of belonging. The scary part of being cared for is the extreme vulnerability that comes with it. I can barely handle it on most days, but I'm trying.

Over the last few years, I have had a close friend renegotiate his level of commitment to me and my family. Relational renegotiations are normal and necessary in any long-term relationship, but the challenging part of this one is that it came with an intimacy downgrade on his side. This is not the same as neglect or abandonment (despite feeling that way at times). This redefines what "cared for" means. A renegotiation ultimately reestablishes what "belonging" will look like moving forward.

In close relationships, when one party wants less from the friendship, it can be extremely painful. New lines are drawn, a plethora of feelings must be felt, and ultimately, the party on the losing end is left to work through the change toward some kind of acceptance for a new normal.

I have been starting to practice both being cared for and caring for others. This is no easy feat for a self-preserving, self-sufficient fighter like me, but at least I am in the ring. It is amazing to start noticing how suspicious and apprehensive I can become when someone cares about me. Regardless, I am on a mission to learn how to both better receive and better give.

Hurt

I had to sell you on being cared for before we could really explore this next feeling: hurt. Oh man, what a vulnerable feeling! It actually took me months and months of checking in with others before I was brave enough to show up to this feeling.

"Tell me I hurt you," invited a friend. "Just say it, Rob. Say, 'You hurt me.'"

It was painfully obvious how this person's actions could have hurt me, yet this friend could see my disconnect and drew me out of my emotional cocoon to feel what was happening so I could name it.

Side note: Because my friend and I had learned the same emotional language, it became a lot easier to vocalize the specific feelings we had with one another without fearing that the world would come to an end. This is one of the most pervasive benefits of learning to "speak heart" in a friendship or workgroup.

I think all people have certain core emotions that are more tender, more loaded with baggage from the past, and as a result, they are more likely to dissociate from. Hurt is one of mine. I have pulled on the thread over the years to explore the reasons for this, but that's another story. It's enough to notice that I will trade the feeling of hurt for just about any other option. And I'll try to interpret my hurt through the lens of another feeling to mask it.

How many leaders do you know who openly confess to feeling hurt? It could be hurt by another person or hurt because of a circumstance. Either way, saying you feel hurt is deeply vulnerable; it's like exposing a chink in your armor that others might exploit. Better to suck it up and lick your wounds later when no one is looking.

Shadow. The potential shadow of feeling hurt is *resentment*. And the feeling of resentment can be easier to identify than hurt for many. Think about that friend who pulled away, that parent who abandoned you, or that boss who fired you. Resentment is the kindling for *revenge*; the next destructive step after resentment.

If children get hurt, adults tend to get angry. Anger is the socially acceptable diversion of hurt for most of us. Anger offers a more aggressive option than being "hurt like a baby," so it's easy to trade in the vulnerability of pain for the perceived strength of hostility. Resentment poisons the soul while revenge lashes out against the one we feel hurt by in an attempt to punish the offender.

Dodd's work on hurt was helpful for me in learning to normalize a feeling I have spent my whole life trying to avoid. "Resentment is the product of trying to find solutions that reject hurt. When hurt is denied, minimized, or projected onto another, it becomes resentment. Through resentment, we are able to deflect the focus from the internal pain and onto someone or something else. This impaired expression of hurt kills relationships and, therefore, stops all healing."[51]

Resentment reminds me of my experience with splinters as a kid. The wooden floors of my grandparents' farm in the remote mountains of South Africa were genuinely rustic. Not the modern refined rustic style so popular now; these farmhouse floors were truly rough and treacherous for the bare feet of running children. A careless dash would catch a splinter and bury it deep in the tender flesh of your foot.

The pain would take your breath away, but if you confessed to Oldman or Grannie, you knew what was coming. They would reach for a needle, which was as terrifying as the splinter, grip your foot firmly, and proceed to pry out the offending sliver. No child understands this to be an expression of love at the moment. So instead, I often tried to ignore the intrusion and move on with life. And we all know how that story ends.

Infection, puss, increasing pain . . . until I couldn't even put weight on that leg. Sometimes, I would even change the way I walked to prevent triggering the pain. So whether the pain is physical or emotional, untreated hurt festers.

Gold. The golden side to hurt rises when you dig deep for the courage to name your pain and bring attention to it in a healthy way.

In his book, *The Voice of the Heart: A Call to Full Living*, Chip Dodd explains it this way:

Hurt exposes our desire to find healing for our pain. The acknowledgment of pain in turn awakens us to our true state as dependent, striving, trusting, curious, spontaneous, truthful creatures who prize life. Ironically, the admission of hurt acts as the catalyst for relief and healing of emotional and spiritual pain. Healing evokes and requires an admission of our vulnerability. Sticks and stones do savage our bodies, leaving us physically scarred, but it's the words that devastate our hearts.[52]

I have to say that my newfound willingness to recognize and express hurt is becoming a valuable attribute in my leadership. It's rare that I feel close enough to pull someone from the business front aside and say, "Hey, you hurt me," but at least I now know the feeling and can process it constructively. And with that awareness, I can lean into the situation rather than let it fester.

In the next chapter, we're going to explore the final quadrant of emotion: the "Soul of Heart" feelings of sad, calm, and lonely, then look more closely at how to invite emotion into our inner transformation. Keep leaning in. I know this is a lot but you're gaining altitude by the minute, and as you do, it will invite practices that will deepen both your performance and your quality of life.

CHAPTER 6

FORMING YOUR FEELINGS

*Feeling and longing are the
motive forces behind all human
endeavor and human creations.*

ALBERT EINSTEIN

LISTEN TO SOME OF TIM'S STORY . . .

Growing up in my house, I was a sensitive kid. A
passionate kid. I remember playing baseball, and
when I struck out, I would throw a tantrum. I felt
angry, sad, and ashamed. Like I was a failure at that
moment, putting all this pressure on myself, and
then I would retreat to the dugout. I remember a few
specific times when my dad would say, 'Stop acting
like a girl and get back out there.' So I internalized
that disapproval and that sense that I was not okay.

These kinds of experiences led me to really silence
my own voice when things got serious. If I felt

something, I was immediately cognizant that the feeling was probably not welcome. I had to keep it under control. So I felt emotions, of course, yet I had zero language to talk about them or desire to. It was unacceptable to express anything that might disrupt the fragile stability of our family; if you did that, you were shamed even more. If I ever cried, I was asked what I was doing, and the message was crystal clear: Emotions are out of bounds. We are a strong family. Be a man!

When my parents separated and eventually divorced, I have a last memory of us all being together one last time—my little brother and my dad, my mom and me. My dad was trying to play a song to my mom over the sound system, but within seconds, she got up and walked out of the room. We're all left sitting there in our living room with this song that had tons of emotion in it. And I think it represented all the unspoken emotions that had littered our home like land mines, all the feelings we had so carefully avoided. We just didn't have any language for it.

And at that moment, it was obvious to me that my mom couldn't handle her feelings either. The man she had just divorced was trying to win her back through a song. Talk about awkward! The emotions were powerfully present, but we couldn't talk about them or process them. Instead, we defaulted to action. We never stopped long enough to get in touch with the feelings that guided those actions. We didn't have time to feel; we just had to figure things out with our heads and do the best we could. If we could stay in motion, then maybe we could dodge the scariness of what was going on inside of us. Now I realize just how broken that was and the terrible cost we paid for it as a family.

As we enter our final set of core feelings, I'm reminded of a statement from Richard Rohr, "If we do not transform our pain, we will most assuredly transmit it."[53] How true.

None of us escapes childhood unscarred by painful experiences. And as we see in Tim's story (and our own), those unspoken rules about how emotion is handled—or not handled—mark us deeply. It usually takes us into adulthood, if ever, to get enough distance from ourselves to understand how the narratives we've internalized have affected us, the relationships we hold most dear, and even the ways we lead.

My purpose for this book is to provide a simple model, practical tools, and a shared language so we can stop transmitting our pain to others, reclaim our feelings, and change the storyline for the businesses and families we lead. We can't write a perfect story, but we can most definitely write a healthier one.

This final set of core emotions lies in what I call the "Soul of Heart" quadrant. These are feelings that connect directly

WE CAN'T WRITE
A PERFECT STORY,
BUT WE CAN
MOST DEFINITELY
WRITE A
HEALTHIER ONE.

with our sense of meaning and identity, and as such, they carry a melancholic tinge. From these power tools of the soul, we feel either grief or comfort, apathy or engagement, isolation or connection. I think you'll agree that this is a potent toolbox for relating and leading.

Sad

Americans are sad. In 2014, one out of four Americans experienced a depressed mood, yet during 2020 as the coronavirus pandemic spread, the number doubled to show that literally half the population suffered from a depressed mood.[54] That's an epidemic within a pandemic.

Sadness can feel like a wet, heavy blanket that presses down on your chest and dampens your soul. Few of us enjoy feeling sad; it's usually brought on by some form of loss, disappointment, or anxiety. It's like heavy clouds rolling in over the sun, blocking out joy and hope. These experiences often lead us to withdraw or distract ourselves, even to medicate the pain we are feeling.

I expect the following exchange will ring true for you.

"How's it going, Andrew?"

"Oh, I'm okay. Thanks." Andrew purposefully limits and withholds the truth while gauging whether the party gathering will allow for *connection* . . . or be limited to *contact*. (You must be careful about reaching for connection in a contact-based environment.)

"I heard you have a lot going on at work," one of them responds.

"Well, yeah. One of my coworkers is vying for the same promotion I am. She made some hurtful accusations about my character that aren't true, and I'm really struggling to gather myself."

Feeling some empathy from the group, Andrew continues. "I've actually been sick to my stomach, having a hard time sleeping, and honestly, I just feel so sad and hurt. I'm struggling to find much joy in life right now. I didn't even want to come here tonight even though I knew I needed to be here with you all. Truth is, I'm really struggling."

Andrew put himself out there, only to find discomfort masked by levity. "Dude! Way to bring down the mood. Grab another drink and wash away your troubles." He tries to laugh it off, caught in what Brené Brown calls a "vulnerability hangover."

In general, Americans aren't any better at holding the sadness of others than they are in holding their own. We generally try to manage grief and loss by solving it like a puzzle or dismissing it as an inconvenience.

Shadow. The fear we often have around sadness is that the shadows of self-pity, lethargy, and depression will set in. If I let myself feel sad about this, what if I never come back? What if it overtakes me?

We use the word "but" to try to bounce ourselves out of the feeling: "Yeah, Lisa was one of my best friends at work, and she left the company last week, *but*, you know, life goes on." In ways like these, we try to buffer ourselves from the feelings of sadness. And in so doing, we lose out on the golden gift within it.

What if Lisa was your only true friend at the company? You are losing someone who matters to you deeply in a place where you spend fifty-plus hours of every week of your life. This is true loss. If you can't allow yourself to be sad and move toward the gold that sadness offers, chances are you'll become withdrawn, isolated, and dabble with self-pity. Feeling alone and abandoned on any level without confessing and processing your core feelings invites the shadow to take over.

"Why doesn't she care about me the way I need her to?" Andy was mad, bouncing between self-pity and blind hope. "My mother is detached. She rarely calls, barely has a relationship with my children outside of the efforts I make, and I don't know what else to do. I am in my late forties now, and it's emotionally exhausting to keep wanting and hoping. Why do other people have parents who reach and connect with their children? Why did I pull the short straw?"

Andy's disappointment and sadness are crippling him at home and at work. He becomes apathetic and sometimes feels pathetic. He can't shake the feelings of hurt, loneliness, and sadness that leak out. Relationships with parents carry enormous equity in our lives. If we can learn to grow our emotional intelligence within our family system, we can overcome in just about any other arena. Families give you the training grounds to become a "special ops" EQ leader.

When you notice yourself internalizing a lot of *whys*, you can assume self-pity is nearby. *Why is this happening to me? Why doesn't anyone like me anymore?* Self-pity means sadness is the likely culprit. If you tell people to stop feeling sorry for

SOMETIMES WE NEED
TO SIMPLY ACCEPT
THAT LIFE HURTS
BEFORE WE CAN BEGIN
TO DRAW MEANING
FROM IT.

themselves, you do nothing more than shame them, driving them even deeper into the shadows. If you instead ask them what they are sad about, you may be able to uncover the area of loss they have experienced.

In 1969, Elisabeth Kübler-Ross first identified the phases of dying in her transformative book *On Death and Dying*. She coined the five stages of grief many of you are familiar with. Denial, anger, bargaining, depression, and acceptance offer a pathway to help us work through loss. I have found that denial, anger, and bargaining are all attempts to avoid our sadness. While depression and self-pity can be the common shadowed effects of our sadness, the golden opportunity is *acceptance*.

Gold. Andy had been experiencing the first four stages of grief in his relationship with his mother for decades. I invited him to consider accepting his sadness rather than fighting it. "Can you name and accept the things you can't change about your mom? And the things you wish she was, but isn't, for your sake and the sake of your children?"

Andy hesitated. Naming his sadness might open the door to acceptance. Eventually, Andy did take this powerful step of owning his grief and accepting reality. It took about two years, but it has revolutionized his life. He still often feels sadness about this core relationship, and he should. It's a small nub of its potential. Despite that, Andy can now live out of acceptance and move forward without dismissing the healthy desire behind the disappointment.

David Kessler, grief expert and coauthor with Elisabeth Kübler-Ross on the iconic *On Grief and Grieving*, adds a sixth stage: meaning. "Many people look for 'closure' after a loss . . . [but] it's finding meaning beyond the stages of grief most of us are familiar with . . . that can transform grief into a more peaceful and hopeful experience."[55]

I don't believe all sadness offers us a great sense of meaning (at least on this side of eternity), but eventually, it can help us think more holistically and comprehensively. And this added stage of meaning cannot be considered until after acceptance. Sometimes we need to simply accept that life hurts before we can begin to draw meaning from it. The temptation for me, at least, is to try to find meaning during my bargaining stage, as in, *I'll only accept the pain* if *I can find adequate meaning in the pain.* Which only holds my healing hostage for another day.

Deep acceptance, true acceptance, helps us loosen our grip on control and lean into a more pervasive trust that—in some form and in some way—all will be well. Acceptance helps us surrender to the reality of being human and embrace a more transcendent hope.

Calm

Calm is an inner sense of peace. When we are truly settled in our skin, we can access this feeling. Even the word itself is calming. Say it three times slowly while breathing deeply. *Calm. Calm. Calm.* Ahhh . . .

Calm is a feeling that can be practiced and intentionally placed within our emotional arsenal for use when needed. It can also emerge in moments we least expect. Learning to access an inner calm in the hardest of moments invites us to experience clarity, perspective, and peace. Grace under fire.

When your first baby is pitching a fit, you can't help but make it about you. *What's wrong with me? Why can't I do this? Am I a bad person, a bad parent? I don't know what I am doing. Oh no!* These voices ratchet up our anxiety and ratchet down our self-worth.

By the time you have your second, third, or fourth child, you don't take it so personally. You have gained more perspective, more levelheadedness, and somehow, you find yourself feeling calm despite the tyrannical manifestations of your toddler.

Calm says, *Yes, the moment is hard (or this client is hard), but I can sit in the tension somehow without it bowling me over.* A humility rises about what we can and cannot do about our circumstances. Calm is not the denial of hard; it is the acceptance of hard. Leaders can learn to access their knowledge, experience, and breathe in ways that help bolster the feeling of calmness.

The Twelve Step framework provides a path for all of us to practice calmness. Step one is the confession of our powerlessness and that life is unmanageable to some degree. Step two brings us into the surrender of a power greater than ourselves that can restore sanity (calmness). Step three is the decision to turn our will and life over to the care of God as we understand God. That's not a bad start.

Shadow. The shadow side of calm is *avoidance* and *apathy.* My wife was convinced as a young adult that she had the superpower of being calm under difficult circumstances. Even as a child, she was praised for how calm she could remain in the face of a storm. The truth that became more apparent as an adult was that this skill was helpful, but it was also a coping mechanism for dissociating and detaching from her own wants, needs, and desires.

It was a simulated calm, and at times, a counterfeit calm. It was a way of putting on the soldier's uniform to fight for the greater good of others—at her own expense. Natalie's calmness was a way of shutting down and taking her Core Self offline. When chaos emerged, she would numb out and check out.

"If you had asked me how I was feeling, I wouldn't have been able to tell you. Abandoning my Core Self allowed me to claim enough serenity to negotiate a ceasefire in our home. And as a young woman, that was compelling motivation. Unfortunately, it took me a long time as an adult to change gears and use my gift in ways that honored both my soul and my environment."

Gold. The golden opportunity that emerges when we feel calm is *clarity*, and clarity contributes toward helping our bodies experience levels of *peace*.

How many great decisions have you made when you were frantic, apathetic, or avoidant? We are often forced to make decisions under pressure, but rarely can leaders make clear, strategic evaluations without feeling some sense of calm. Within in the pressure cooker, we must access a peace that surpasses understanding to be healthy, Heart-Engaged leaders. This is part of fighting for our hearts.

Dale was a childhood friend—an ocean man who sailed yachts and took tourists out for cruises in the Atlantic and Indian oceans around Cape Town, South Africa. Over a beer

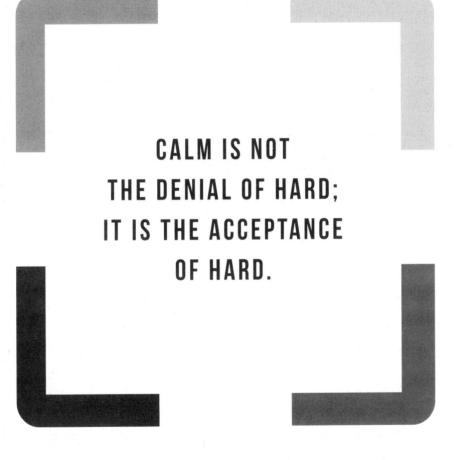

CALM IS NOT
THE DENIAL OF HARD;
IT IS THE ACCEPTANCE
OF HARD.

and pizza one night at the Red Herring, he recounted one of his sailing stories from the old days.

Dale had a group of about twenty out for a sunset cruise when, instead of serving champagne, they were met with a squall that emerged from nowhere. Within minutes, crew and passengers were in a fight for their lives, moving quickly from excitement to terror.

Like all good sailors, Dale recounts the event as if it were just one among thousands of tales already recorded in his memoir. Among the panic and screaming, one passenger grabbed him by the collar and yelled, "You need to call someone to help us! You need to call someone to help us!"

Dale's response was a classic mixture of calmness, competence, and seasoned experience. "Ma'am, you need to calm down, I am your help! Now go sit down, be quiet, and I will get you home safely."

If there is one person I would want in a storm, it would be Dale. As captain, he was not only confident but also calm, despite the dangerous conditions. Moments like these were not new for him; he knew how to recognize danger but also how to harness emergency strategies with logic, trusting himself and his crew. That's what the feeling of calm can accomplish.

Calmness invites clarity. As leaders in all kinds of industries, we are learning to be responsive and not reactive. Trustworthy leaders aren't tossed back and forth by calamity but instead focus with commitment on the greater good. With the gold of this emotion, we can see clearly and steer a good course, even in a storm. Just like Dale.

Lonely

Most Americans experience loneliness. We have more knowledge, resources, and credit lines to build our little kingdoms than ever before, yet the spaces we create often feel void of intimacy. I often consider how the average home today offers more luxury than kings and queens enjoyed a thousand years ago.

"Today, three in five Americans (61%) classify as lonely, according to results from our latest research based on the responses of more than 10,400 adults in the U.S."[56] And loneliness may be on the rise. The report, led by the health insurer Cigna, found a nearly 13% rise in loneliness since 2018, when the survey was first conducted. "More than one out of ten lonely workers say their work is often (*most of the time or always*) lower quality than it should be. On average, lonely workers say that they think about quitting their job more than twice as often as non-lonely workers."[57]

Yes, the results are in: America is a lonely country. Social isolation is at an all-time high (accelerated by the COVID-19 pandemic) and is generating significant health trauma, amplifying relational distress, and marginalizing the human experience.[58] To make matters worse, loneliness is one of those feelings that carries a stigma.

Not many of the executive leaders I work with are willing to admit they are lonely, and yet it is blatantly obvious they are. Not only are they lonely, but they are lonely to be with. The cure for modern-day loneliness is activity and distraction, so we bloat our schedules, only to find that this makes the loneliness worse. Activity is one ingredient that can support connection, but activity alone is not going to solve the problem.

Many of the guys' gatherings or social events I attend are fun, loud, and noisy, but it's common to leave feeling less known than when I arrived. We may do stuff together, which can be awesome, but there is less and less time and space to go beyond the doing. Even four hours of golf leaves you little more than a few crumbs of connection between shots and looking for balls in the woods. Americans are becoming less known, and it's hurting us. Could the confession of loneliness and connection with a tribe become a strategy for turning the tide on the loneliness epidemic?

I had seasons of significant loneliness strewn through my childhood that have continued to affect me through adulthood. At the dinner table last night, I asked my family if they had any stories about feelings of loneliness.

My seventeen-year-old son, Noah, asked honestly, "Don't you have plenty of your own stories to share about that?"

Everyone else concurred.

I was caught off guard, but it was good to feel known without being shamed. My children are learning to normalize and humanize emotions; our conversations are becoming more connective and meaningful than I could have imagined. As a result, loneliness is no longer a shameful feeling at our dinner table but rather invitational, even when it is mine.

You likely live and work with people who make you feel lonely. They see you to the degree that you work the plan, but beyond company objectives, you are mostly unseen. The dutiful "care question" a boss may ask in passing is not sufficient to overturn how lonely it is to work for that person. What do you do with that?

Shadow. The shadow of unrecognized loneliness leads us toward *withdrawal* and *isolation.* If you are lonely with someone for an extended period and your efforts for connection are exhausted, withdrawal becomes the next viable option. You pull back and retreat to your own fortified castle. In a marriage, that might look like separate beds, separate interests, separate friends, and indifference to one another's needs outside of the agreed-upon housemate arrangements.

In the marketplace, loneliness can drive you to curb your desire for connection altogether, pushing you to become more of a lone ranger. You clock in and clock out, living your best life after hours with other people. And while this kind of independence may be rewarded in the corporate culture, that same culture risks eroding the very heart we all so desperately want and need to make our companies great.

We are communal beings; there's no escaping it. When we withdraw from others, we fight against our inherent design. Heart-Engaged leaders learn to recognize the defense mechanisms of withdrawal and isolation, and then formulate strategies for connection as a roadmap back toward people. We can't force it, of course; sometimes, people aren't interested in reaching back. But healthy leaders learn to read themselves, read others, and forge heart connections when possible. This is the essence of emotional intelligence.

When people are unwilling to respond to our invitations

for connection, we have to renegotiate the relationship accordingly, which may likely include accepting disappointment and grieving the loss of what you had hoped for. This takes work, to be sure, but don't kid yourself: Self-preservation and withdrawal take a lot of effort as well. Don't let the shadows of loneliness keep you from living; don't let them shut down your heart.

It's also important in this age to be aware of the counterfeit connections we call social media. While promising to enlarge our sphere of relationship, they skew the very quality of connection we hope to achieve and often leave us lonelier than ever. Virtual connection easily slides toward addiction, salving our itch momentarily, only to inflame it the moment we log off. No, the connection we truly long for is only met in real-time personal interactions. Which leads us to the gold of loneliness.

Gold. The gold of loneliness is *connection* and *solitude*. I always thought I hated solitude until I realized I was just afraid of being abandoned. There are notable differences between being alone, lonely, abandoned, or isolated. Revisiting these expressions and experiences in your story can help outline steps you can take towards both connection and solitude. When we cultivate a quality and substance of life marked by heartfelt, intimate connections, we start to carry an innate groundedness wherever we go. In fact, authentic solitude actually amplifies the magical connection we can have with ourselves and others.

I used to joke, "I am going to get some alone time now.

Do you want to come!" These days I am becoming more comfortable and even desirous of solitude. When I feel safe and connected to myself and my core relationships, it gives me the trusted foundation to venture further out on my own. This is new territory for me. I will likely never achieve the depths of solitude that come easier to my wife, but I can say that learning to voice my loneliness and reach for connection is unlocking the treasure of solitude and community in beautiful ways.

Loneliness is now a helpful register for my current level of attachment to those I want and need in my life, along with the impetus to reach for more. Recognizing and working through your loneliness will enter you into the top tier of emotionally connected leaders out there today. What if we could change the tide and help establish Heart-Engagement as the new norm?

Noticing for Formation

Now that we've unpacked the vital essence of the twelve Core Emotions, we have a shared understanding and common language to talk about what's in our hearts. We've explored how to use these essential parts of the human experience as a bridge to connect our hearts to the hearts of others, whether in our home, the workplace, or the community.

This changes everything.

Three emotions from the Mind of Heart: *Afraid, Confident,*

and *Lost*. Three from the Strength of Heart: *Angry*, *Excited*, and *Guilty*. Then the Heart of Heart: *Ashamed*, *Cared For*, and *Hurt*. And finally, the Soul of Heart: *Sad*, *Calm*, and *Lonely*. Here's a chart that summarizes the shadow and gold of each. The big twelve are a great place to start exploring. And sometimes, we can back into the core feeling by noticing which gold or shadowed expression is showing up.

anxiety & control	**AFRAID**	*discernment & refuge*
arrogance & carelessness	**CONFIDENT**	*action & purpose*
vulnerability & desertion	**LOST**	*discovery & gratitude*
aggression & force	**ANGRY**	*advocacy & action*
sensationalism & deception	**EXCITED**	*infectious joy & energy*
blame & punishment	**GUILTY**	*forgiveness & freedom*
self-contempt & escapism	**ASHAMED**	*humanness & help*
codependency & powerlessness	**CARED FOR**	*belonging & interdependence*
resentment & blame	**HURT**	*attention & courage*
self-pity & lethargy	**SAD**	*acceptance & hope*
avoidance & apathy	**CALM**	*clarity & peace*
withdrawal & isolation	**LONELY**	*connection & solitude*

No longer must we swim in a sea of churning, nameless emotional currents. We now have a simple and clear way to parse out the language of the Heart, work through the shadows, and reach for the gold. As you do, here are three things to notice about how you instinctually engage feelings. And as with anything new, remember that it sometimes gets worse before it gets better.

First, *notice which feelings you admire, default to, and encourage in others.* Some feelings are more comfortable than others, so we tend to overdevelop those (intentionally or unintentionally) at the expense of the rest of our emotional palette. But as we start paying attention, we'll begin to recognize how often those feelings dominate and sideline the others.

Anger is a common culprit for many. Anger is more socially acceptable and feels more powerful, so it's easy for anger to cloud the softer feelings of being afraid, sad, or hurt. Shame is another loud voice on the bus; many feel bullied by the feeling of "not being enough." Sadness can be another elevator feeling that operates from a place of self-pity and victimhood. Excitement and sensationalism can be front-runners for those who make constant attempts to avoid anything hard. You may be driven to chase the next high and avoid the next low.

Recognizing your go-to feelings helps you become aware so you can then push deeper and explore the whole gamut of feelings you avoid, suppress, or dismiss, which we do for a variety of reasons.

Second, *notice which of the twelve feelings you look down on or avoid at all costs.* If you could quieten your inner noise, what feelings are alive and well but more muted or dismissed? What are the stories and circumstances that silence them? Feelings have a way of making their way out in the real world, whether you accept them or not, so why not get curious before they come out sideways?

Hurt and cared for are suppressed emotions for me. I struggle to access the feeling of hurt due to a combination of factors—nature and nurture—in both my personal and professional histories. Hurt or the lack of feeling cared for suggests weakness, and weakness suggests being shamed or cast aside. I hate the notion of being powerless or feeling like I need something. Hence, these vulnerable emotions feel like enemies. Now, however, hurt is becoming one of the most empowering and strengthening emotions in my toolbelt, unlocking courage and connection with others more than ever before. Who knew?

Third, *notice the feelings that tend to show up together.* Not only do we have a relationship with each of the twelve, but the feelings have a relationship with one another. Often, two or three will "clump" together on a somewhat predictable basis. This is a tremendous opportunity to learn the wiring of your heart and become more fluent in the language of heart.

Very rarely does a feeling exist in isolation. For example, the feelings of excited and afraid are often tied together in some way. Excited suggests action, and action means putting yourself out there in a way that almost always carries some level of risk and fear. Maybe you are feeling lonely at the office but notice emotions of shame and lost nearby. Guilt and shame are clear companions, although they are sourced quite differently. You get the point.

When you can access the full scope of all twelve feelings in your life, then you're ready to notice patterns that offer a more comprehensive expression of your current experience. Emotional processing goes to a new level when we not only understand each feeling, but also have the freedom to access and express them.

Practice Your New Heart-Language

We have explored twelve feelings that offer a cohesive language to access your heart in a more connective way. It's a lot, I know, but you've just been equipped to navigate life and relationships like never before.

Here is a simple practice for putting this new awareness into practical action:

- Every day, pull out a piece of paper and for ten minutes, write down as many feelings that feel real for you at that moment, regardless of the reasons, context, or accuracy. Say them out loud as you write them. Speaking makes our feelings become more real. "I feel . . ."
- In groups we say, "Thank you for sharing" after the initial check-in, so why not say that to yourself? It's

a way of validating that your confession of being human is a gift to yourself and to others. It's also a way to start rewiring those sneaky beliefs that feelings are bad and should be avoided.

- With your feelings identified, now isolate two or three from the check-in and start expanding on each. Try connecting to the feeling. (Remember, you can tear up the paper and throw it away afterward, so give yourself permission to expand the scope of each feeling). If you checked in with excitement, for example, start writing about what you are excited about, what you hope and fear around this feeling, how it's impacting you, and so forth. Exhaust that feeling, and then move on to the next.

- Having honored the experience of your feelings, you're now ready to explore the golden opportunities and shadowed threats each can bring. Identify a step or two that will help you reach for the gold.

- Close your time.

At first, this may feel like a waste of time, but stick with it, keep showing up, and keep practicing. Heart smart is very different than head smart, and that's why you're reading this book.

In my next chapter, I'm going to introduce you to the four characters that animate the heart. Now we're starting to get some exciting synergy in this quest to be Heart-Engaged.

CHAPTER 7

MEET YOUR CHARACTERS

Unity, not uniformity, must
be our aim. We attain unity
only through variety. Differences
must be integrated, not
annihilated, not absorbed.
MARY PARKER FOLLETT

I WILL NEVER FORGET my first few months of inviting mentors to help shape my leadership journey. Not advisors, who are fairly easy to come by, but rather, sages who have embodied the very principles and practices they share. My partner, Jack, and I are two very different human beings. Considering age, nationality, history, and leadership style, we are almost opposites, but that's exactly what makes it a great relationship for us. We share a congruent vision and sense of calling about guiding leaders through the deeper pathways of change and transformation in their lives, and working together makes us better.

In one of our earlier meetings, he uttered these brief but

loaded words in the midst of one of my passionate *Let's-change-the-world* filibusters: "Rob, you do know that you've made it, right?"

I paused, confused.

"You made it," he continued. "You have survived your life. Can you see that? Do you believe that?"

His perspective challenged my view of myself. What could it look like to let the survival parts of Rob take a back seat to my story? What could it mean to allow some new, expressive parts to show up and chart my course into the future?

Jack was trying to help me think about the "parts" of my life and their influence. He knew how ruthlessly I had adapted and trained to be hypervigilant and stay one step ahead of danger. These survival tactics had served a necessary purpose before, but they were now starting to limit my emergent potential as a man and leader. Jack was inviting me to recognize, honor, and discharge my "survivor," so I could begin to live a more creative, responsive life. Perhaps for the first time.

Who are the characters that shape the landscape of your life? How do they express themselves in your leadership? A leader who's driven by survival can be extremely effective at achieving certain outcomes, while at the same time, deeply hindered by others. I have always known how to pick up my sword and fight my way through, which often meant accidentally wounding others in the process. But if all I do for the rest of my life is to fight and survive, is that really living? It's certainly not a life of abundance.

So rather than shaming and blaming the characters who

have carried my story, what if I could honor the important role that the Survivor has played, release that character to take a break, and finally welcome others to shine and build the next season of my life? This is the opportunity each of us faces right now. The names of the characters may be different, but the dynamics are eerily similar within our human sojourn.

Emotionally aware leaders are those who are able to recognize and explore the characters that drive segments of their life and leadership. We are meant to be curious and connected to all the parts of ourselves. Integration is the process that unblends and differentiates these parts, so we can move unhindered along the Contact-Communicate-Connect-Commune pathway. While I try not to lead primarily as a Survivor these days, I still invite that character to sit at the table and have a voice when appropriate. This is the skill we want to learn in this chapter. First, let's recap what we've talked about so far.

Step one of the Heart-Engaged EQ System taught us how to catch up to ourselves and become more centered (chapter three). Step two taught us how to check in with what we are feeling and better understand the shadow and gold of twelve core emotions (chapters four, five, and six). In this chapter, we will introduce you to step three: the four primary characters that bring texture to every person's inner world.

Much like feelings, we could name countless characters. But I have identified four that will function like primary colors to help us explore and align together around a shared language and understanding.

The conceptual inspiration for the Core Characters section of my system comes from an amalgam of several research influences that have crossed my path over time. Before you get concerned that I might be suggesting you have a multiple personality disorder, let me briefly offer you two theoretical frameworks that underpin this content.

Internal Family Systems

One framework comes from the work of Richard Schwartz, PhD and his Internal Family Systems (IFS) paradigm. Although primarily used in therapeutic environments, I have found tremendous value in contextualizing some of his work for the leadership arena. Schwartz designed a metaphor that helps us visualize the various "parts" of our being that are interacting in various capacities and has categorized them into three primary roles: *Exiles, Managers,* and *Firefighters.*

Exiles are the more tender parts of ourselves who have possibly been wounded or dismissed. As a result, they are relegated to the basement where we hide them from everyday life and leadership. You may refer to these parts as your "baggage." Exiles usually remain locked in the basement of our consciousness. We are usually ashamed of them and try to keep them hidden. These vulnerable parts of ourselves carry much of the pain, hurt, and fear we have picked up along the way.

The ground floor of this personality metaphor is governed by our *Managers.* These parts of us are tasked with the job of protecting our Exiles from the harsh real world. Managers are empowered to care for them while projecting an image of normalcy. The last thing we want is our "dirty laundry" out in the open, so our Managers work proactively and strategically to help us keep it all together.

Meanwhile, our *Firefighters* reside on the top floor, always on standby in case the Managers fail to keep our Exiles protected and controlled. When our carefully constructed version of normalcy and competency crumbles, Firefighters are the 911 responders, ready to jump in and put out the fires by any means necessary. With little regard for consequences, they power in to rescue our Exiles and whisk them off to safety, buying time for our Managers to recover and reengage the world with a semblance of stability.

The intent of both Managers and Firefighters is noble. They seek to mitigate threats and pain, and attempt to relieve you from the burdens of your life and leadership. Unfortunately, they tend to do this in ways that are often forceful and controlling, which may cause collateral damage in your relationships. It's fascinating to start to recognize the exchanges among these three groups within the inner workings of your life.

The IFS system is "a highly effective, evidence-based therapeutic model that de-pathologizes the multipart self. IFS has become an effective framework for helping move individuals through various challenges and trauma by identifying, ordering, and considering the various 'parts' that exist within us. Richard defines IFS at its core as a loving way of relating internally (to your parts) and externally (to the people in your life)."[59]

One of the prime perspectives of the IFS model is that there are *no bad parts* of us. There are just parts trying their best to take care of us in their own ways. This approach invites us to be gracious and compassionate with ourselves— even the dynamics that feel broken or dysfunctional—so we can better integrate our Core Selves and exert a more positive influence. Schwartz encourages us to believe that "our parts can sometimes be disruptive or harmful, but once they're unburdened, they return to their essential goodness. When we learn to love all our parts, we can learn to love all our people—and that will contribute to healing the world. . . . On the other hand, if we hate or disdain our parts, we'll do the same with anyone who reminds us of them."[60]

You, Inc.

I created this next framework to offer a contextualized and approachable metaphor for leaders. I like to picture a corporate setting where there is a CEO, Messengers, Managing Partners, and Key Performance Indicators (KPIs). And these roles correspond to the four steps of my EQ system:

- The Core Self (step one) is the Owner CEO.
- Our Core Feelings (step two) are our Messengers.
- Our Core Characters (step three) are the Managing Partners.
- And our Core Outcomes (step four) are our Key Performance Indicators.

Let's build this out a little more.

Your Core Self is like the **Owner CEO** of You, Inc. You steward a deep sense of why you started the business, how you hope to run it, and where you hope it will go. You are the majority shareholder and the sole voice who can overturn and overrule those who work within your emotional organization.

Meanwhile, your Core Feelings are **Messengers**. They are the twelve voices of emotion that support and inform the CEO and the Managing Partners. These messengers are coming at us from both within and without, interpreting the landscape in order to guide, warn, gut check, inform, affirm, protect, direct, and influence your emotional system. They are not always accurate. In fact, they are sometimes skewed or compromised, yet in many cases, they are spot on. Regardless, they deliver a steady stream of intel that good CEOs and Managing Partners must learn to invite, interpret, and process, or they risk flying blind.

The Core Characters we're about to study are the four **Managing Partners** of your EQ operation. They have part ownership of your life, working for the Owner CEO in ways that can help interpret the Messengers and bring emotional leadership for strategic planning, decision-making, policies, budgets, partner relations, emotional performance, risk, etc. These four Partners manage your emotional business, and each has its own vested interest in how they do so. Like all managing directors, there are times they bump into each other (and the CEO) as they go about accomplishing their tasks. We'll unpack these roles more in a moment.

The Core Outcomes are your **KPIs**, and we'll learn about those in the next chapter.

When all four team members of You, Inc. are locked and engaged, it's a thing of beauty. Your life's vision is inspiring. You feel in sync with yourself. Your plans for how you want to live, love, and lead move forward with intentionality. All of this is deeply satisfying. With CEO, Managing Partners, Messengers, and KPIs each in their place, You, Inc. flourishes. Emotions may fluctuate with circumstances, but your sense of identity, purpose, and function generates both quantitative and qualitative returns.

Peter has always been a fiercely competitive and determined leader in each of the companies he has worked in. "No" was never an option and, as far as he was concerned, second place was the first loser. And he was no loser. The competitive and determined parts of Peter have served him well in corporate America, helping him climb the ranks of every team.

Despite these exhilarating strengths, it was terrifying to be on Peter's team. He carried an energy and drive unmatched by those around him, and you knew you had to give 250 percent to win or you'd find yourself another team. Failure was not an option for Peter, even though failure is baked into the human experience. His team would sometimes forget whether they were working to build the company or to pacify Peter's ambition.

But it's impossible to hold the pole position in all things, so when things went bad, as always happens eventually in the real world, it got ugly. Competitive Peter became Abusive Peter and Medicating Peter. He would shout and rage his way out of the office, driving straight to the neighborhood pub to camp out and blow off steam with countless drinks. His family would wait at home wondering when, or if, he would make it back. But inside You, Inc., one of the Managing Partners became Medicating Peter, and he figured he deserved temporary relief from the pressures of his job and the pain of his failure. And that meant drinking.

What is known to a few people in Peter's life but not Peter (a Blind spot in the Johari Window) is that his competitive, determined Managing Partner (and his self-medicating firefighter) are working to suppress Peter's past, insulating him from facing and integrating historical wounds. He hates these Exiles.

At age fourteen, Peter felt so rejected and abandoned by his parents that he woke up and vowed he would never be a "loser" like his dad or "helpless" like his mom. Longing desperately to be loved, he struggled to cope with the brokenness of his family that left him bleeding on the inside. So he did what he had to do to survive and locked up those tender, vulnerable parts of his younger self to try to silence and surmount his past. But it never actually works that way. Only when the pain is faced, the feelings are heard, and the Core Self is integrated can healing and wholeness return. Otherwise, we simply lock ourselves in a tower of our own pain and transmit that pain to others we love while we power up the ladder.

What Peter is beginning to learn through our work is that every child deserves to be loved. What he wanted as a child was healthy. He is also learning that the way he has tried to manage and extinguish the pain of his exiled past is understandable but doomed. Instead, he must cautiously invite his Exiles out of the basement of the past to be healed in the present. Perhaps he can learn to lose without being a loser. And perhaps he can learn to trust and collaborate with others without considering himself helpless.

The hard work is starting to pay off.

Peter's wife now says their home feels different. Better. The people on Peter's team say they can breathe more deeply around him. Peter still loves a good competition, but it doesn't define him as much anymore, and he's more considerate of others. And as he gives voice to his Exiles, he is noticing them grow up; his need to force the win is decreasing. He's learning to perform out of the love of the work rather than trying to prove he's worthy. He's even picked up some past clients who are relieved to work with the less controlling Peter 2.0.

Have you ever taken inventory of the characters in your life? It's not that easy until you know what to look for. And even then, it's helpful to have someone outside of your own context to assist. I highly encourage you to do this, and in the next pages, I'm going to give you some tools to do so.

Introducing the Archetypes

I love this part of the EQ system because I latch on to story and imagery much easier than facts and figures, especially when it comes to matters of the heart. I find it much easier to see myself through the lens of these four composites. Archetypes offer us a more tangible picture of our emotional world in the often intangible and even complicated world of emotion. In particular, they help us access the heart in the domain of commerce and community.

In this section, you'll meet four primary characters that offer a textured visual of your emotional system. They are neither intrinsically good nor intrinsically bad; instead, each carries both a golden and shadowed expressions that will impact you and those you love positively and/or negatively.

You may find yourself noticing certain behaviors around your emotions that suggest the active character(s) at play in your life and leadership. Everything is connected. The Core Characters will deepen your emotional intelligence by helping you recognize and access the influences that dominate various parts of your life. In time, you'll be able to identify and relate to each character in varying capacities, engaging all four in strategic and purposeful ways to help you fight and lead from the heart.

Let me introduce you to The General, The Trailblazer, The Caretaker, and The Mythic.

ACTION

feel-less   *feel-out*

GENERAL

Detached, Dismissive, Paranoid,
Harsh, Aggressive, Controlling,
Committed, Assertive, Responsible,
Expressive, Balanced, Patient.

TRAILBLAZER

Impulsive, Reactive, Erratic,
Abusive, Unpredictable, Abrasive,
Bold, Adaptive, Effective,
Courageous, Curious, Resilient.

REPRESSING

EXPRESSING

feel-in   *feel-more*

MYTHIC

Indifferent, Superiority, Distant,
Impatient, Cryptic, Unreliable,
Grounded, Discerning, Enlightened,
Creative, Accountable, Reflective.

CARETAKER

Unsettled, Anxious, Seductive,
Demanding, Enmeshed, Resentful,
Considerate, Compassionate, Caring,
Expressive, Empathetic, Intimate.

ATTENTION

The General

This character kicks in to get your emotional life under control by lowering the intensity of your feelings. The General helps you feel less, which can be either a positive or a negative outcome, depending on the situation.

When emotions run high and hot, the General shows up on the scene to enforce emotional order and bring calm to the chaos. *This character's central contribution is to use practicality, reason, and logic to defuse complex or vulnerable emotions in you and others to create emotional stability.* This character represents the Mind of your Heart, so you can consider this the rational side of your emotional system.

Emotions are tolerable and even useful when the General is active, but only to the degree that they can be transferred into positive action. This character uses pep talks and instruction to help you surmount challenges.

When did you become so emotionally stoic and practically minded? I often ask the leaders I work with. "My General kicked in strong around my teen years" is the common reply.

For many, the General shows up early in life to protect. It's the moment when life is hard, and the only option is to show up, buck up, and climb up out of hardship with courage. For others, this character appears in the late teens or early twenties when their biology starts to naturally trend toward independence and self-sufficiency outside the childhood home.

Here's how Joseph's story played out.

My dad was strong, bold, and aggressive while my mother was more creative, whimsical, and unpredictable. Given my own disposition, it made sense to enlist my General so I could survive and thrive under the leadership of my dad the General. Together, we were a force to be reckoned with. These militant characters brought structure and direction to my insides. Connection? Not so much. As a result of this character's influence, I realized over time that I had become tougher, but this came at the cost of indifference to my own and others' emotional needs.

It has taken a lot of personal work to honor this character in my life, and then right-size it. As I am learning to unblend and integrate, I feel more connected both at home and work. I need my General to lead well, but I am engaging this part of me in ways that feel healthier and more constructive now.

As we will see, each of the four primary characters in our inner lives serves a vital purpose, but through our personal narrative, it's common for one to overdevelop and overtake the others, with the effect of marginalizing our emotional intelligence. This is the particular benefit of naming and identifying the characters: We learn to recognize how each has shaped our story in helpful and unhelpful ways and begin to invite these four voices into greater collaboration and cooperation. This begins with understanding the Gold and Shadow that each character brings to the table.

Shadows. The less helpful influence of the General is to make you feel *detached, dismissive,* or even *paranoid* so you begin to act out with *aggression, harshness,* and *control.*

When these negative attributes dominate, leaders may suppress their emotions to power up, anesthetizing awareness of how their behaviors may negatively affect those they lead. You detach from and dismiss objections in order to shore up your own sense of confidence. You might find yourself becoming irritable, critical, or patronizing toward anyone who exhibits what you consider to be "emotional weakness."

The General in you can become machine-like—over-committed to technical outcomes, while negating the feelings that drive connection and intimacy. This character drives productivity and performance. At its worst, the General becomes both heartless and defensive, injuring others while shielding the self from return fire, all for the sake of masking insecurity and driving an impersonal but validating agenda.

Beth unloads part of her unreconciled story with me. "My mother was not the most affectionate woman to grow up with. She will likely go to her grave believing she did a great job as a parent because she put clothes on our backs and food on the table until we were eighteen. She was a good provider and fierce fighter in those early years, but sadly, I don't remember the last time she hugged me or even asked me how I was doing in a way that felt real."

We all have moments of enlisting the General to help us manage our emotional states. This can be necessary and even helpful at times, but the challenges emerge when those moments turn into months, years, and eventually decades. When this character is hyperactive or over-prioritized, physical and tangible needs are elevated above emotional ones. Quantitative above qualitative. Services delivered instead of hearts connected. Activity instead of Attention. Head over Heart. Doing over Being. Your other characters can get intimidated and shut out of the conversation. Given too much bandwidth and stage time, you can expect the shadow side of the General to harden your heart.

Some days, you will wake up feeling ambushed by some of

the feelings in your life. The shadowed General works hard to cut those feelings off at the knees so you can charge out the front door as if nothing were wrong. Long, hard workdays are a welcome distraction, a medication even, in these moments or seasons; in fact, the General welcomes and justifies them. But when you come home at night, it's hard to shake off the detachment and hang the uniform in the closet to transition back into the role of loving spouse, parent, and friend. So the General attempts a split life—becoming one person at work and another at home. Eventually, it fails at one or both.

If you work for someone with strong General tendencies, you may often be shamed or dismissed. You may feel afraid to share your personal life, knowing he or she will either coach, correct, or cut you off. Your feelings may be tacitly acknowledged but then trumped with a playbook reminder of the company mission and objectives.

You may hear something to this effect, "I know George is going through a brutal divorce, and I really care about him, but at some point, he's going to need to pull himself together. I went through the same thing, but I never let my personal life affect my performance at work. He really needs to come back to reality."

This statement seems fair but notice the "but" and the shaming comparison. It may be true that if George doesn't find a way to navigate his divorce his job may be at stake, but could there be a more caring way to position the relationship than dismissive shame? You'll need another character to pick up the dialog at this point.

Yet the General has shining moments too. Let's look at those.

Gold. A healthy leader can differentiate between thoughts, feelings, and behaviors. And since the General is the more rational and logical part of the emotional system, when this part of you kicks in, you are empowered to navigate a path through emotional complexities to reach for sound direction and leadership. That is a valuable and necessary commodity—one we call *emotional regulation.*

"Nearly all psychiatric disorders include one or more primary dysregulated emotions (e.g., anger in borderline personality disorder, sadness in depression, fear in anxiety disorders, shame in narcissistic personality disorders, etc.). Thus, the ability to regulate emotions adaptively is essential for well-being."[61]

So in addition to emotional regulation, what is the positive potential of the General? At its best, this character is committed, assertive, responsible, and expressive. When leaders tap into the genius of the General, they become more confident and decisive, more patient and balanced while keeping their eye on both organizational and relational goals.

Leaders who can process their emotions in decisive ways can be extremely attractive to employers, and healthy Generals may find themselves elevated and rewarded through the strengths of self-awareness or emotionally intelligent communication.

Under the influence of healthy Generals, you will be invited, and sometimes pushed, to become stronger and climb higher in your own life, pushing through limiting beliefs and toxic shame that cripple confidence. Healthy Generals are emotionally predictable, dependable, logical, and productive. They provide a sense of safety for those who work under their leadership.

While other characters bring varying levels of adventure, unpredictability, or complexity, you know what you are going to get with a Golden General—a sturdy anchor, a trusted foundation. When Generals are living out their healthy expressions, they will be emotionally competent, strong, and dependable. Life will be hard at times, but you find yourself grounded. I like my General when he is living out his gifts.

The Trailblazer

This character activates emotional intensity that drives energetic action. Determined to *feel out*, the Trailblazer dials up feelings of adventure, change, and innovation in their quest to generate movement. This can be a scary-exciting character to have at the table, which also makes this the most turbulent of the EQ cast.

Representing the Strength of Heart dynamic—the more visceral side of your emotional library—*the main goal of the Trailblazer is to harness the emotional fuel to propel you forward into new territory.* This rocket thrust tends to come with more intensity than intimacy; relational connection is more the domain of our next character. In the meantime, buckle up and enjoy the ride.

I have considered myself a "feels good, let's go" kind of person, which gives my Trailblazer plenty of stage time in my life. Yet I am also learning to be more intentional in deepening these expressions within my emotional system. Remember, the shadow of feeling afraid can make you more controlling, which usually signals my General to kick into gear. To counteract that tendency, I am reaching for the gold of the Trailblazer to become more exploratory and adventurous around the things I fear.

Growing older comes with wisdom and gray hair, cautioning us against foolish risks. Age can also lull us to sleep with comfort and predictability, such that life becomes underchallenged or boring around the midlife mark. For many, their Trailblazers have been tamed, governed, and domesticated, leaving little to instigate healthy fear and excitement. Weekends blend into monotony, eating out is no longer as special, vacations are placed on a checklist, and so forth. *Is this it?* you wonder on another Friday night in front of the TV.

Some of us need to defibrillate our Trailblazers back to life and dial up the heart rate. Do something outside your comfort zone; put yourself in situations that force you to grow. Jump out of an airplane, say yes to the next ten questions anyone asks you without knowing what they will be, or commit to doing one new thing you have never done for seven days in a row. Feeling anxious? Good. Your Trailblazer is waking up and joining the table.

Shadows. There are, of course, downsides to this character. At its worst, the Trailblazer can be impulsive, reactive, and erratic, creating chaos for yourself and others. Sort of an emotional ADHD that can become reckless. When the unhealthy Trailblazer grabs the wheel, it's a stormy adventure, scattered and sporadic, chasing shiny things and taking uncalculated risks.

You will never know which version of the shadowed Trailblazer is showing up today, which puts you on your back foot. You'll have to work hard to process the fears or resentment that can arise when following a leader who over-relies on this character. Trailblazers may utilize affirmation and encouragement, but they may come across as disingenuous or manipulative. When this character runs wild, it becomes oppositional, demeaning, abrasive, and even abusive, leaving tire tracks across the face of anyone who gets in its way.

Adam, an account executive, describes growing up with Trailblazer parents. They were passionate and emotional yet simultaneously turbulent and unpredictable. It was feast or famine, fear or fantasy. He doesn't remember feeling safe or secure during the heightened emotional experiences of his family life.

"What's wrong with you, Adam? You're so withdrawn. Get more excited." Maybe it was his dad losing another job that dimmed his excitement. Or maybe it was the eventual bankruptcy, living with other families, food stamps, and church programs. Maybe it was going to the umpteenth new school. What was projected by his parents as a fantastic adventure (to survive their own lives), Adam finally came to understand, was actually a series of traumas that left him reeling and insecure.

He felt alone, confused, and different. The narrative spun by his parents clashed loudly with his own internalized truth.

It has taken years for Adam to unblend the gold and shadows of his Trailblazing parents so he can unearth a more honest relationship with himself and with them. Now he recognizes when that character in their story tries to commandeer him into some new "adventure" he doesn't want. In these moments, he can access the healthy side of his General to bring reason, strategy, and autonomy to the situation without feeling abandoned and without stifling his own sense of adventure.

In the office, the shadowed Trailblazer can be extremely intense to work with, and while intensity can be useful to power through projects with focus and determination, that intensity can also become oppressive when demanded of others. You realize you are holding your breath when you're around this person, always waiting for the other shoe to drop.

I have come to realize that I can be a pretty intense leader, and my focus can be aggressively narrow at times with both assets and liabilities. If I am set on pushing through my own feelings to deliver results, it's easy to under-access the concern, empathy, and calmness that nurtures connection with those I am working alongside.

Another potential downside for the shadowed Trailblazer is vision trauma, in which every week brings a new and different objective than last week. These leaders make ninety-degree turns without warning, leaving their followers with perpetual whiplash. In self-preservation, such followers will either stop listening or jump out of the car.

In social settings, people with strong Trailblazer traits are passionate, inspirational, and sometimes domineering.

Especially when these parts collude with the General, you can expect demanded intensity. Imagine yourself hanging out at a party and having a good time. The night is filled with casual laughter, good wine, and funny stories. Eventually, you realize it's getting late. You have an early morning and need to go home. You start to move toward a subtle exit when the alpha in the group speaks.

"You're not going home, are you?"

You've been called out publicly for trying to leave quietly. You love that your presence is wanted, but this feels more like control. In the awkward moment, you backtrack and stay a little while longer until you use the restroom distraction as an excuse to ghost the party.

Now let's look at the golden side of the Trailblazer.

Gold. At its best, this character is curious, bold, adaptive, and effective. With courage and focus, Trailblazers, well, blaze trails. They can be an exciting addition to a relationship, project, or community.

The healthy Trailblazer is inspiring and inviting, always looking for new ways to do things and new places to go. They are catalysts for excitement, bringing energy and charging the atmosphere. Feelings are welcome with this archetype and often invited. A simple comment such as, "I like your shirt" could be met with, "You do? Here, have it." Kindness without manipulation comes easily for the healthy Trailblazer.

Despite not always being organized or strategic, this character's passion inspires others to follow their dreams. You can think of this part of you as the extraverted expression of your emotional system. Particularly in the workplace, the environment easily becomes sterile, devoid of vitality and celebration. It takes your inner Trailblazer to waken the dead, renew camaraderie, and attract others to the mission.

Montana Brian is one such leader. He heads up an organization that serves and cares for leaders, and hundreds have experienced his team's hospitality over the years. With generous hearts, they set the table for hosts like me to bring small groups into the wilderness of Montana and Wyoming where we fish, shoot, ride, feast, and hang out together.

Brian has a Trailblazing energy that fuels the hearts and souls of weary leaders. The trip combines fun with outdoor adventure that awakens those who have fallen asleep in their jobs, buried by responsibility. The trip alone is not transformational; it's invitational. It's an opportunity to recover your heart so that meaningful growth can occur. This is why we need Trailblazers.

I have been working hard over the last few years to strengthen the positive attributes of my own inner Trailblazer. I realized one day how serious I was, how little adventure and excitement I felt on any given day. Midlife doldrums? I don't know, but I made a conscious decision to place myself in environments that would force me into more risk and activity.

Last summer, we had just arrived at the neighborhood pool with all the kids. I'm not sure exactly what happened next, but I pushed my wife into the pool with all of her clothes on and joined her seconds later when one of my kids pushed me in fully dressed. We all exploded with laughter and splashed each other in fun. What was the point? No idea, but one of my kids brought it up again the other day, reminding me of how much more exciting it is to have a little unpredictability in my life, even in simple ways.

Are you safe, predictable, apathetic? What can you do to reawaken your adventurous heart and feel your blood pumping again?

The Caretaker

This character in your emotional system seeks to serve, love, and care for others. Those who lead with this character find these actions instinctive; it's what they do, who they are, or perhaps what they feel compelled to do to feel worthy. The Caretaker represents the Heart of your Heart and with its *feel more* orientation, it embraces emotion as the essential means for connection.

At the heart of this character is the intent to ensure that people are going to be okay, that they will be accepted and included, not emotionally orphaned. This motivation lands somewhat at odds in the famously strong and self-sufficient stereotype of business leaders. Many corporate men and women are more comfortable projecting strength and power while desperately covering their natural needs and vulnerabilities.

The Caretaker assumes two distinct roles, yet at its best becomes a both/and rather than an either/or.

Caretaking for self is the first important role of this character, often learned through seeking attention or helping you live without it. It's vital to have healthy self-care lest we polarize in the opposite direction and over-focus on the care of others at the expense of self.

Caretaking for others is the other means by which this archetype offers comfort and purpose. Caretakers feel responsible and significant when they help people in emotional distress. And the reciprocal appreciation and love that flows back validates and fuels their efforts.

"I care about people to a fault," Steven confided with me. "I wish I could turn that part off sometimes because it's exhausting. I am constantly seeking out new ways to make sure everyone is okay. To do this job well, I have to be vigilant and attentive, searching for opportunities and making calculated predeterminations of what people want and need." Steven, like so many other leaders, believes he's okay if you're okay. If there is peace in the village, then there can be peace in his soul.

As a middle child of two working parents, he was always overlooked, so he learned early on the necessity of making himself valuable. His older brother was the sports guy, and his younger sister was the demanding one, so Steven figured out that the only way to get praise and attention was to alleviate the pressures of his parents. Every time he took care of them, they would affirm his considerate nature and commitment to the family. This felt good, so he kept doing it.

Caretaking is often learned at a young age for a host of reasons. Without a safe place to develop a healthy Core Self, a person's identity easily becomes enmeshed with others.

They frequently detach from their own emotions, wants, and needs in order to be more available to yours. The risk for Caretakers lies in losing themselves (codependency) when tethered to the emotional responses, opinions, and behaviors of others. And therein lies both their gold and their shadow.

Sometimes, while working with a group of executives, I encounter a particular leader who stands out from the rest. He or she holds a significant position yet appears to lack the respect of some colleagues along with the commensurate confidence in the role. When I pull back to observe the landscape, it may become apparent that this leader plays a significant caretaking role for the leader in charge. This leader has been pulled up the ladder to offer care, comfort, and emotional support to someone, often a General. The opposite of this shows up in some family businesses in which the owner is driven by his or her inner Caretaker to ensure that children and family members will be kept safe and sound in the madness of commerce.

Shadows. The dysfunction in the unhealthy Caretaker emerges when one's safety and value are contingent on the constant need, gratitude, and dependence of recipients under your care. As a result, the shadowed Caretaker is often experienced as unsettled, anxious, seductive, and demanding.

"Elliot, you fight harder for deep relationships than anyone I know, which is often awesome. But I also find you suffocating, which pushes me away. I think you care about others because you are driven by your own childhood wounds of not being cared for. You want people too much, and I believe you use me and others to meet all those emotional needs. Not everyone wants the same thing from relationships as you do. I hope you can get that."

This painful criticism came from a close friend as the relationship was being renegotiated later in life. The accusation felt gut-wrenching and seemed irrecoverable. Despite the harshness in the exchange, I was able to help Elliot catch up to himself by taking a lap around his four quadrants (step one). As a result, he saw himself more objectively and recognized some deep truths in his friend's words—truths that awakened newfound awareness.

Committed to his emotional growth, Elliot used this uncomfortable situation to take inventory of his life. It became clear to me that both Elliot and his friend were using opposite strategies to accomplish the same objective. Both wanted to be safe and cared for, but while Elliot's tendency was to pull people closer, his friend's strategy was to keep them at bay.

Who's right in the civil war between needy and needless? Usually, nobody is completely right; long-lasting relationships require us to keep showing up for one another, despite our differences. When one or both parties refuse, the relationship will unlikely survive the winter.

When the Caretaker's need for approval leads to codependency and enmeshment, the internal dissonance sometimes works itself out in ways that feel compulsive, overbearing, or resentful. A recent study found that "the experience of codependency, according to participants, [is] manifested through difficulties in living a balanced existence, suggesting a perceived lack of internal stability. Participants all related their lack of self-definition with continuing occupational and emotional unmanageability."[62]

Corporate codependency can be more subtle, but no less shadowed. Jane describes it this way: "I work for a company in which the owners are highly emotional, deeply caring, and slightly controlling, all at the same time. I started working there in my early twenties and was drawn to the feeling of family. What I never realized was that I had given away parts of myself in big and small ways to become a 'daughter' in the organization."

Like all of us, Jane longs to belong, and when a workplace environment offers some form of invitation and relief from the neglect we experienced at home, it's natural to lean in. Over time, however, Jane found herself letting go of her boundaries and, eventually, most of her identity. She learned that if she vigilantly cared for others in the organization, they would, in turn, care for her, and she would not be so alone. She made a new "family," and the unspoken contract was that unreserved loyalty would be rewarded by being treated like a daughter.

The owners were inadvertently saying, "We are taking care of you emotionally, financially, and spiritually. We expect you to never leave us or grow beyond us without our expressed permission. If you ever try to leave us, we will have no choice but to defensively reject you." These are not actual words, of course, but this is actually how it played out.

Seeking bold steps to grow in her career and even pursue a new industry, she was met with fierce resistance from the company. To protect their own emotional security, they tried desperately to keep their "child" from growing up by becoming controlling and resentful. That's the downside.

Gold. The healthy side of the Caretaker is a dramatic capacity to see and care for the needs of others without neglecting the needs of the self. Motivated deeply for relational harmony, this character is the glue that holds teams and families together, salving wounds and conveying worth. They are considerate, compassionate, and expressive with the intuitive ability to empathize with authenticity.

The Caretaker values and seeks relational intimacy. He or she carries a unique talent for creating such intimacy, as we saw in both Elliot's and Jane's stories. Dan McAdams defines the need for intimacy as a "recurrent preference or readiness for warm, close, and communicative exchange with others—an interpersonal interaction perceived as an end in itself rather than a means to another end."[63]

Intimacy is a stranger in most workplaces, so when it arises in healthy ways, it is indeed powerful. "The capacity for emotional intimacy—a greatly undervalued capacity—is essential not only to truly fulfilling relationships, but to having an uncommonly vital life in which awareness, passion, love, action, and integrity function as one."[64] This ethos, when used for the empowerment of others and not to restrict them, can transform fractured workplaces into vibrant, caring, close-knit teams.

The Mythic

This character represents the Soul of your Heart that manages and expresses the complexity and comprehensiveness of your emotional experiences. *This is the feel-in character in your emotional system, probing the depth and meaning that lies hidden underneath the feelings themselves.* While the Mythic may not drive productivity and action, he or she serves a vital role for leaders who are seeking to gain altitude in their emotional worlds.

Ever feel flooded by emotions? Life has a way of ensuring that we get emotionally overwhelmed from time to time. Some may even say triggered. When this happens, it's easy for the Trailblazer to fan the flames, the Caretaker to medicate, and for the General to manage or shut down the party altogether, but the Mythic offers a wiser, more centered alternative. When hundreds of internal data points converge, bouncing around like pinballs inside a noisy machine, this archetype offers a way out. The Mythic brings a calming sense of perspective to the madness and helps us understand that, while we may be having big feelings, we are not our feelings.

Dave describes it this way: "When things get hard and complicated, I always know that I can sit down with my friend Peter to get some perspective. He helps me access the calmer, more curious sides of what I am feeling and going through, rather than throwing a pep talk or plan my way like others often do. Peter has something I can only describe as deep presence and clear awareness.

"Just a few months ago, I had been struggling through some complexities with one of my anchor clients, and it was coming to a head inside of me. Someone on my team had made a mistake, which only further escalated what I was feeling. Tired, frustrated, anxious, and angry, I was rethinking my career altogether. Extreme, yes, but a lot had been mounting with this client and the industry. 'Peter, I am done. I don't want to do this anymore,' I declared at the table over a meal together. 'I am in the wrong business, and I want out.'

"Instead of affirming my conclusions or matching my energy, Peter simply responded with 'Dave, you're upset. Before you go blowing things up, let's keep looking at this. I want to ask you to wait four weeks before making any decisions about your role in the company. Are you willing to commit to this challenge before taking action?'"

Peter had come to learn that when healthy leaders are in crisis, they need to slow down the intensity in order to access the emotional treasures found in the Soul of the Heart, for themselves and others. Healthy leaders create space to calm down, process their feelings, and uncover clarity that makes for better decisions.

Not every situation requires four weeks of waiting, but in this instance, Peter listened to Dave and knew he was right. Four weeks later, Dave met Peter to thank him for his guidance and to report that he was not only staying with the company but was seeking a promotion to a position from which he could address some of the systemic issues that were plaguing him. Peter's emotional intelligence wound up saving Dave's job. This is the Mythic at its best.

Shadows. At its worst, however, you may find the Mythic

managing your emotional world with distance or indifference, detaching to rise above, or even floating away from your problems. These might be decent short-term strategies, but it's only a matter of time before your Trailblazer or Caretaker jumps in to set your emotions free by bleeding out or blowing up. That's always an entertaining event, so bring out the popcorn.

The impaired Mythic often carries an air of superiority, impatience, or coldness, as if he or she sees the situation more clearly than anyone else. While this can be true, it fails to recognize that *seeing* feelings is not the same as feeling them, leading with them, or harnessing them for good. This Blind spot can make the Mythic unreliable and inaccessible in certain situations.

Manipulation is another interesting shadow of the Mythic. Those who are highly aware of their feelings are often aware of others' feelings, which gives them some power to partner with the General and do damage. Ever felt like you were being played by someone at work?

Some books and seminars teach people how to use relational strategies to win people over in the recruiting process. You feel flattered by the attention you're getting, only to realize it's part of a big play to lure you. Should you refuse the closing invite, you'll be met with instant rejection as the Mythical General moves on to the next recruit.

I am learning to be more truthful with my intentions to oust the destructive potential of my Mythic around the emotions of those I am leading. It's subtle, but eventually, people will learn whether you value them for their own sake, or if they are simply chess pieces being moved around on your board.

Gold. Mythic gold often comes in the form of grounded-ness, enlightenment, and discernment. Its capacity for reflection yields high insight and creativity, making this a valuable force at the internal table of emotional intelligence. The healthy Mythic assigns meaning and context to your feelings so you know how to interpret them wisely. At its best, this character is a faithful servant who welcomes and extends accountability.

Listen to John's experience of seeking a healthier experience of his inner Mythic.

I grew up in a home with an over-functioning, emotionally charged mother and an under-functioning, emotionally distant father. Mom ran the emotional show and I quickly realized that I preferred avoidance like my dad so that I could keep an even keel. This approach felt way safer and less invasive.

Looking back, I realize I abandoned myself as I pretended everything was fine and dandy, regardless of whether things truly were. When life got hard, I found ways of ignoring or limiting my emotions so they never went too high or too low. I diluted the intensity of feelings by actually slowing my heartbeat. Relinquishing both advocacy and anger, I learned to avoid the risk of exerting power or demanding things from others (like my mother).

More recently, I'm learning how to open my heart and trust that it can have a voice without being overbearing. My hypervigilance as a child has been repurposed to be self-aware of my emotional content, which is making me a wiser and more discerning leader.

This is the gift of the Mythic in action.

Managing Your Characters

As we close this section, take a moment to pause and reflect on how these characters are showing up in your life right now. You should recognize something of yourself in all four, and you may notice certain feelings connected to one character and other feelings connected to another.

Your General may be working to cast a vision for your team and require more accountability, while your Caretaker may be reminding you to invest in the health of the team culture. Your Trailblazer may be urging you to put your passion in motion, while your Mythic may be beckoning you to a personal retreat for reflection. All these voices are necessary and useful when they cooperate without domination.

Under emotional stress, it's natural to look for someone or something to blame, but the blame game is merely a distraction. Emotionally intelligent leaders don't respond to hard relationships or conflicted situations with a witch hunt. *Instead, they learn to create space between the stimulus and their response.* This is the key.

In this space, a healthy leader can check in with themselves in microseconds, listening to the parts that are being triggered—both the parts that are over-functioning and those that are under-functioning. And they notice the patterns and recognize which voice is needed to be productive and purposeful in response. *To respond rather than react.* They can then move with emotional clarity, scaling their leadership to communicate and act in the most constructive manner, regardless of who's at fault.

The goal of the emotionally healthy leader is to be centered, awake, and engaged. Learning how to consciously recognize the four characters and how they affect you is vital for a Heart-Engaged leader. Learning these voices will grow your EQ and make you more effective in every facet of your world. Here are a few pointers to aid the journey:

1. Expect to have characters who are favored and over-function and, as a result, are easily triggered.
2. Expect to have other characters who under-function, hide, or are dismissed as useless.
3. Expect to find character alliances who collaborate to protect your emotional equilibrium by any means necessary.

Start noticing. Get curious. Tune your inner observer as you respond to different kinds of situations, and over time, you'll see the patterns emerge. It's hard to leverage the potential of your emotional gifts until you discern the unique voice of each character at the table, and learn which is most appropriate in the moment.

Very few of us want to be flooded with emotions in the marketplace, but without emotions, the marketplace becomes a ruthless machine. How can we learn to navigate these complexities? By practicing the Heart-Engaged EQ System. So far, you've learned to check in with your Core Self (step one), name your Core Feelings (step two), and respond to your Core Characters (step three). The final step is to choose your Core Outcomes, and that's where we're headed next.

As my friend Donald would say, "Now we're cooking with gas."

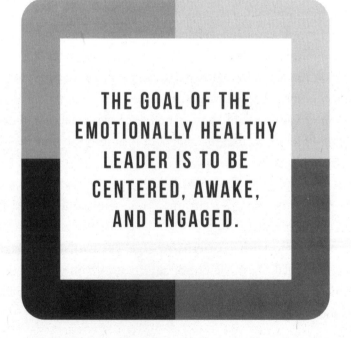

THE GOAL OF THE
EMOTIONALLY HEALTHY
LEADER IS TO BE
CENTERED, AWAKE,
AND ENGAGED.

CHAPTER 8

OUTCOMES & PAYOFFS

The emotional brain responds
to an event more quickly
than the thinking brain.

DANIEL GOLEMAN

YOU CAN'T WAKE UP IN THE MORNING and decide to become a more emotionally intelligent person by lunchtime. And no one tries until he or she first believes in its potential . . . and has exhausted him or herself with every other strategy. The leaders I meet often realize they want "more," but they're not sure what "more" is, or how to find it.

So let me be clear, this is the "more" you're looking for: your heart.

I have come to believe that what leaders are missing most, and searching for most desperately, is their heart and the connective power that the heart brings. We are tired of isolation at home and at work, tired of fleeing our own emotional history, and tired of the hollow meaninglessness that heartless work brings.

Our souls have been managed away as line items in the budget, and that's not working anymore. Humans are creatures with body, soul, mind, and yes, heart. We have feelings, and those feelings are meant to be one of our greatest treasures, not a liability. It's time to change the narratives of emotions in the workplace, not to mention the home, and then find the skills to harness their potential.

That's why, standing on the shoulders of many before me, I have created the Heart-Engaged EQ System. My hope is that we can gain the perspectives and tools to change the story and reclaim our lives as emotionally intelligent people. As we do, we'll gain countless benefits along the way.

Investing in the internal essence of your leadership is a commitment to a lifelong journey. And as we know, every journey is made of a series of steps, one after the other. Before we get carried away with this fantastic vision, I'm not kidding myself: Not everyone will step into the beautiful, messy world of the heart. To feel is to welcome both pain and pleasure, connection and alienation.

Research shows that all humans are searching consciously or unconsciously to live fully human,[65] but most will struggle to take their first steps for a variety of legitimate reasons. Try telling the survivor of abuse to simply open his heart and feel his feelings. Or try telling the project manager who lost her last job because her divorce bled into her performance that year.

There are reasons why most of us have bottled up and

ALL HUMANS
ARE SEARCHING
CONSCIOUSLY
OR UNCONSCIOUSLY
TO LIVE FULLY
HUMAN

buried a portion or even all of our hearts to stay safe in this complicated world. Regardless of our history, we face an all-important choice. Will we be defined and forever limited by the wounds of the past, or will we integrate and transcend our past for an emotionally healthy and relationally connected future? This is the poignant opportunity and decision we face today.

The western mindset in particular is very practical and logical, leaving little room for things like dreams, stories, and feelings. We instinctively process our past to avoid a recurrence of pain in the future. Few will casually step into the growth I am advocating unless there is a provocation. And usually, that reason is some kind of mounting failure that eventually reaches a critical mass and forces us into a new way of looking at ourselves and the world around us.

Every good movie delivers an inciting event that summons the lead actor to get off the front porch rocking chair and face unsurmountable odds for the hope of glory and redemption. Yes, I am specifically talking about *Rambo 3*, but it's the same all around. Something or someone has to shake your life enough to draw, pull, or push you into starting the mission.

I hope you will be left with a pebble in your shoe from what you have read, and that this pebble will make you walk awkwardly enough to invite you to stop and make a real choice. Will you engage in the journey of becoming a more emotionally engaged leader? Will you let your exiled emotions out of the closet and listen to their sage voices? Will you build new bridges to the people who matter most to you?

Some will see the title of a book like this and run for the hills. Others will buy it to learn how to solve a particular EQ problem. Some will be intrigued because they are looking for a courageous frontier of growth. And still others (like me most of the time) will hunger for a genuine path toward more meaning, substance, and connection in the ways I live, love, and lead. Whatever your motivation, I welcome you to move toward a life of significance by re-engaging that which makes us most human. Heart.

Real change is possible. Likely, even for those who step onto this path. One of the most encouraging points of my research is that, regardless of the emotional mindset our participants inherited from their family of origin, and regardless of the unhealthy coping mindsets they adopted as a result, every single participant expressed shifting to an emotional healthy mindset after nine months of working with the Heart-Engaged EQ System.[66]

This doesn't mean, of course, that we don't sometimes revert and act out old habits, but a mindset is an underlying value system that begins to shape both identity and behavior. We have tasted something and can't go back. Over time, our actions gradually and inevitably shift to become more congruent with our beliefs, and this is huge.

A Bottle of Wine

Natalie and I celebrated our fifteenth anniversary visiting the Amalfi Coast and Tuscany, and of course, you can't visit Italy without enjoying their wine. Of all the vineyards we visited, one called Nostra Vita stood out by far because of the story of the family who runs it. The father actually hand-paints the labels on each bottle. Truly magical.

If you were to have come to my house over the years, you would have seen a bottle of reserve selection Brunello di Montalcino 2012 from this vineyard on the rack above several others from the local liquor store down the road. All red wine, all somewhat delicious, but the Nostra Vita bottle commanded our attention due to its place in a story that was unfolding. Even the wine itself continued to develop as it aged in its beautiful bottle.

Boxed wine gets the job done, but there is something mystical about a bottle of wine that has been carefully considered, chosen, and laid down for a specific number of years to bring it to perfect maturity. Our plan was to take this bottle to England in the summer of 2022 and open it at sunset in the small coastal town of Woolacombe in North Devon, marking twenty years since Natalie and I met in that same spot. Even writing these words evokes deep emotion as I consider how a simple bottle of wine became the symbol of our maturing love. A symbol of heart. A point of intimate connection. A painting in progress.

So how is your heart doing?

Do you lead with heart or head? Books, conferences, and coaches often pit one against the other, and the trend leans strongly toward the virtues of the head. Quantitative measurements. Hard data. Objective metrics. And yes, these are valuable and necessary but are hardly the whole story. Truth is, we become what we measure.

If you approach the work of emotional intelligence the same way you approach profits and performance, you will struggle. Great leadership requires both quantitative metrics as well as qualitative, and it is these "softer" measurements that give us access to a quality of life worth living and leading. "Qualitative data, although sometimes more subjective and difficult to grasp, are just as real, just as important, and can be gathered just as systematically as the quantitative," says the father of modern management Peter F. Drucker. "Hard work is indispensable to success, of course, in this as in any other field; intelligence is prized in our sector as in all others involving intellectual endeavor; and caring is what has drawn the best people into this line of work. But ultimately what is remembered is how we have been able to improve lives."[67]

As I hope is clear by now, I am an advocate for both head and heart in this battle. The most heart-driven company won't be a company for long without a profit. At the other extreme (and far more common), the most aggressive profit-driven company will undermine its longevity by neglecting the qualitative measures that comprise its culture.

"We hire racehorses and battle horses," one leader confidently tells me. "Leaders who are strong, capable, and dependable. Leaders who surge into battle when necessary and who can survive working longer and harder than their peers." The irony is that they are meeting with me to address their retention issues and inability to find enough "racehorses" in the millennial generation.

If your sole goal is to hire a certain stripe of leader throughout the organization, you are going to succeed with certain measurements and completely fail at others. For this company, their corporate culture is defined from the very top-down by competition, not collaboration. It's not working anymore. What this company has yet to learn is that a robust, thriving enterprise needs not only racehorses and battle horses but also pack horses, trail horses, show horses, ponies, and more. The whole gamut.

I said a moment ago that we become what we measure. According to Dan Ariely in the *Harvard Business Review*, "It can't be that simple, you might argue—but psychologists and economists will tell you it is. Human beings adjust behavior based on the metrics they're held against. Anything you measure will impel a person to optimize his score on that metric. What you measure is what you'll get. Period."[68]

What are most CEOs measured by? Stock prices. The bottom line. So we shouldn't be surprised when all their attention and decisions are driven by the need to move the needle in that direction in the short run. "If you were subjected to such unrelenting scrutiny, wouldn't you do as much as you could to get the number up? Even if you knew your actions would probably come back to bite you in the long run?"[69]

Long-term change will only occur when we can talk freely about the vital interplay between head and heart in the long-term success, quantitatively and qualitatively, of our corporate mandates. And then begin to invest in, and measure, both.

Here's the way Jack and I describe the dynamic in our first book: Although the emphasis may shift somewhat from season to season, there is an intrinsic connection between who we are in our essential identity and what we do in our actions. All "doing" flows out of "being," yet "being" must express itself in authentic "doing." Western culture, and the business world, in particular, tend to over-emphasize the performance side of this equation and damage the "being" side through neglect. Great leaders manage this polarity by attending to both the humanity of their people as well as providing accountability for their work responsibilities.[70]

What's the Payoff?

So far in this book, I've offered you a system—a series of intentional steps—for developing your emotional intelligence. I hope you've found these steps approachable and achievable and are already experiencing the benefits, inside and out. This journey is not so much difficult as it is foreign to many of us. It takes patience and perseverance to keep leaning into the process. Fortunately, the transformation we experience at each stage helps fuel the journey.[71]

So let's talk about outcomes. What is it that we really hope to accomplish through all this heart-work? When I lead cohorts, I ask whether anyone in the audience thinks emotional intelligence is an essential attribute of leadership. Every hand goes up every time. The second question I follow up with is, "If everyone thinks emotional intelligence is vital for leadership, who here is doing something intentional, specific, or strategic to build this part of themselves"? Usually, only one or two hands go up. The gap analysis between belief and action is complete, and the results are typically poor. The third and final introductory question I ask is for attendees to define what emotional intelligence even means. I grab my marker and wait for answers to write on the whiteboard. Usually, three, four, or maybe five answers emerge, but they are spotty, vague, and random. Empathy, the awareness of others, and the awareness of self usually come up consistently, but after they are mentioned, the suggestions slow to a trickle.

At this point, I conclude this introduction with a sobering recap. Everyone believes emotional intelligence is vital, but nobody is doing anything about it, and even if they were, there is no clear understanding of what it is anyways. At this point, I invite participants to consider using the Heart-Engaged EQ System as a resource to lead them into a great understanding of this invaluable gift we have, the heart. We've been talking EQ outcomes for some time now, but in this chapter, I hope to spell it out for you. The following chart outlines the specific metrics of growth I measure in my work with the Heart-Engaged EQ System.[72]

	LOGICAL EQ	PRACTICAL EQ	SOCIAL EQ	SPIRITUAL EQ
ATTRIBUTES	Self-Control	Self-Confidence	Self-Worth	Self-Awareness
BASELINES	Emotional Regulation	Emotional Agility	Emotional Connection	Emotional Perspective
COMPETENCIES	Committed	Courageous	Compassionate	Creative
	Assertive	Adaptive	Authentic	Accountable
	Responsible	Resilient	Relational	Reflective
	Expressive	Effective	Empathetic	Enlightened

These are the specific ways you can expect to improve your life, your relationships, and your leadership on the way to becoming a more emotionally savvy human being. I call them the "A, B, C's" of becoming Heart-Engaged (*Attributes, Baselines*, and *Competencies*). Now I'm going to attach one layer of outcomes to each step of the EQ system.

We started with step one, Catching up to Yourself, where the focus is on leading from your Core Self. As you take that initial lap of connecting to your body, noticing your thoughts, refreshing your meaning, and identifying your feelings, something begins to emerge almost magically. You connect to your body and feel a rise in *Self-Confidence*; you notice your thoughts and release *Self-Control*; you refresh your meaning and get an immediate bump in *Self-Awareness*; and you identify your feelings to find a boost in *Self-Worth*.

These are all fundamental payoffs for growing emotionally. The Self does, in fact, grow with this kind of heart-work, and the result is that you increasingly detach from the automated reactions that governed you in the past. Instinctive coping mechanisms that we defaulted to in our inner world begin to yield to the larger insights now available to us. Now, more options, healthier options, are on the table of possibility.

"Simply bringing simmering feelings into awareness can have salutary effects," says Daniel Goleman. "When sixty-three laid-off managers participated in a study at Southern Methodist University, many were, understandably, angry and hostile. Half were told to keep a journal for five days, spending twenty minutes working out their deepest feelings and reflections on what they were going through. Those who kept journals found new jobs faster than those who didn't."[73]

All your hard work in the EQ gym is paying off, and your Self muscles are growing. Here I go again making workout analogies, with my subconscious shame reminding me to do something about my dad-bod.

It's impossible to have "self of anything" without being on the path to access and express your core identity. Emotional health grows from the inside out. It invites you to recover a deeper sense of Self by aligning your gifts, talents, and behaviors with your deeper design and purpose.

In this section, I'm going to use a lot of descriptors to paint the picture of just how powerful the outcomes can be from doing this kind of EQ work. But despite the plethora of words, the concept is quite simple, and I think the following diagram will help make the relationships clearer.

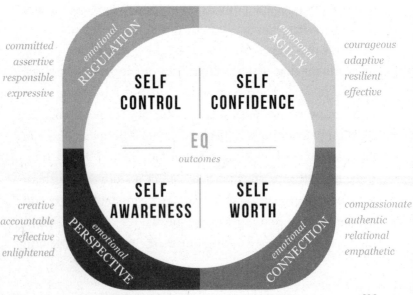

committed
assertive
responsible
expressive

emotional REGULATION

SELF CONTROL

emotional AGILITY

SELF CONFIDENCE

courageous
adaptive
resilient
effective

EQ
outcomes

creative
accountable
reflective
enlightened

emotional PERSPECTIVE

SELF AWARENESS

SELF WORTH

emotional CONNECTION

compassionate
authentic
relational
empathetic

At the center of the diagram (in white), you'll see the four payoffs we just named: *Self-Confidence, Self-Control, Self-Awareness*, and *Self-Worth*, and these are the natural outcomes for leaders who are investing in their emotional intelligence. In the next ring, you'll see a set of baseline outcomes that flow out of the first, and we have identified these to be *Emotional Perspective, Emotional Regulation, Emotional Agility, and Emotional Connection.*

And in the four corners, you'll see four adjectives that best describe the emotional competencies of leaders who are investing in their emotional intelligence, for a total of sixteen desirable qualities we can authentically associate with the Heart-Engaged EQ System. All that and a cape.

I want all sixteen of these, don't you? But like most worthy goals, they rarely appear without intentional, committed steps. So may we be reminded to roll up our sleeves and start reorganizing our time, money, and effort to align with our desires.

Self Confidence

I imagine most of my readers would say that self-confidence is a quality they find useful in life and leadership, and fifty percent of my research participants reported an increase precisely in this dimension.[74] Confident doesn't mean smug or arrogant. Far from it. Genuine humility shows up as confidence when leaders know what they're good at and what they're not.

A few pages back, we said confidence begins with connecting to the body as you check in with yourself. Breathe in and feel an abundance of oxygen rushing into your lungs to sustain you. Our bodies are always conveniently located in the present moment, and when we *feel out* into these physical containers, we automatically loosen our grip on the fears of the future or concerns of the past. We belong to the now, and that bolsters confidence.

As we begin to become aware of our essence, self-confidence begins to emerge, along with the ability to express that value in the real world through emotionally intelligent action. We may recall what has and hasn't worked in the past; we may become aware of resources we need that are available; we may intuit how to sync up the timing of activity with our energy. And the result is confidence.

Norman and Hyland describe the effects of confidence (and lack of confidence) in the educational field: "Lack of confidence made student teachers self-critical and doubtful of their own abilities; anxious, nervous, tense, uncomfortable and insecure; they had difficulty communicating with and interacting with others; and they avoided certain tasks. Increasing confidence on the other hand had facilitative effects. Growing confidence allowed them to adapt to new situations quicker, take on more responsibility, engage more fully in the learning process, enjoy learning, be more relaxed, be more motivated, and interact more easily with others."[75]

When we turn our attention to start recognizing and naming our feelings, both the comfortable and uncomfortable ones, we begin to gain the trust to know that we will be enough and have enough to lead well. Staying in and working with your feelings over time starts to produce **Emotional Agility**.

Agility is the ability to move quickly and easily in response to change or challenge. When you place that within the realm of emotions, you can access your feelings without them burying you, and then see a host of options for responding, choosing the one that promises the best outcomes. That sounds like a leadership superpower to me.

"A growing body of research shows that emotional rigidity—getting hooked by thoughts, feelings, and behaviors that don't serve us—is associated with a range of psychological ills, including depression and anxiety." Expert psychologist Susan David continues, "Meanwhile, emotional agility—being flexible with your thoughts and feelings so that you can respond optimally to everyday situations—is key to well-being and success."[76]

Be careful not to confuse agility with avoidance. Some people may seem flexible but are actually disconnecting from the situation and its legitimate emotions. True agility isn't afraid to look the situation dead in the eye and *move through it instead of around it.*

Heart-Engaged leaders are learning to strengthen their hearts in ways that make them more **Courageous**, **Adaptive**, **Resilient**, and **Effective**. I want to bring particular attention to the quality of resiliency. The quality of resiliency is particularly rare and necessary for a healthy, sustainable life. It requires an acceptance of life's complexities while retaining the conviction of life's meaning. Easier said than done. I often refer to the *beautiful brokenness* of our human condition, affirming both sides of that tension. It's not a polarity as much as a fullness of dimension, and we must live within the full spectrum of this reality for emotional resilience to be forged.

In the *Harvard Business Review*, Diane Coutu posits that "resilient people . . . possess three characteristics: a staunch acceptance of reality; a deep belief, often buttressed by strongly held values, that life is meaningful; and an uncanny ability to improvise."[77] You can see within Coutu's description the marriage of suffering and joy that calibrates our expectations of what life will bring us along with that essential ability to adapt and improvise in the face of adversity.

And when it comes to effectiveness, research has established that teamwork blossoms within the context of emotional intelligence. Within the full orb of heart-informed leadership, there is simply so much more information to draw from, as well as healthier connective tissue from sharing and synergizing that information.[78]

Self-Control

This is the next payoff for those starting to invest in their emotional intelligence. Realizing that emotional distress directly impacts self-control, it's easy to see why this quality would be a treasure trove for the skilled leader. Without it, such turbulent feelings tempt me to zone out with a movie and popcorn, while others seek relief in an aggressive five-mile run. Yet both strategies are a form of self-medication rather than self-control. I gain ten pounds with my strategy, and you destroy your joints with yours. What if self-control was more than either of these?

"Self-control—or the ability to manage one's impulses, emotions, and behaviors to achieve long-term goals—is what separates humans from the rest of the animal kingdom," describes *Psychology Today*. "The richness of nerve connections in the prefrontal cortex enables people to plan, evaluate alternative actions, and ideally avoid doing things they'll later regret, rather than immediately respond to every impulse as it arises."[79]

Muraven and Baumeister also point out that "there are likely to be substantial individual differences in the basic capacity for self-control. In other words, some people have a larger reservoir than others of self-control strength. Second, in principle, it may be possible to increase the size of people's reservoirs over time. If self-control operates like muscular exertion, then exercising self-control may increase strength. Although the short-term effect of exerting self-control may be to deplete and diminish one's capacity, the long-term effect may be the opposite. Frequent exercise of self-control followed by the opportunity for full rest and replenishment may gradually increase the individual's total strength for self-control."[80]

Moving out from the center of the diagram, we deepen our EQ with emotional regulation. Identifying our feelings, whatever they are, and being able to hold those feelings with self-control forges within us the skill of regulating those emotions, directing them in ways that benefit your soul, your closest relationships, and your team.

Emotional regulation is best understood as the ability to keep one's center within strong emotions without becoming overwhelmed, holding dissonance with confidence rather than reactivity until the content can be emotionally metabolized. I have found in my work with leaders in various industries that without a well-developed capacity for emotional regulation, long-term teamwork and effectiveness are severely compromised, which makes sense.

Heart-Engagement will help you channel emotion through the lens of reason and logic for strategic outcomes. These heart investments will increasingly make you more **Committed**, **Assertive**, **Responsible**, and **Expressive**. Like the sound of that? Would these qualities contribute to your leadership effectiveness?

Perhaps you say you already have these qualities, and I believe you. When we described the contributions of the General in the last chapter, we noted that this character is most accepted in the modern leadership culture, so it tends to show up more easily than the other three characters. When it shows up, it brings both the strengths and weaknesses of its voice to your internal conversation.

The quality I'd like to draw attention to here is being *expressive*, as distinct from being assertive. Generals are caricatured as those who are comfortable barking orders at minions who rush and scurry about, putting those orders into motion. And in the heat of battle, you'd better know how to tap into the gift of assertiveness; war is not the time for ambivalence. But expressiveness is uniquely informed by emotional intelligence in these ways.

Heart-Engaged leaders understand first how they are being affected by their own feelings and out of that awareness, they know how to convey their feelings in ways that will have the desired effect on those around them. When we say being expressive, we don't mean venting, yelling, or bullying. Emotionally intelligent expression understands the impact of tone, volume, body language—and all the subtleties that influence how words are received—and shapes those expressions for the most effective outcomes. Now let's look at the next quadrant and its best payoffs.

Self-Awareness

A strong share of participants reported an increase in self-awareness from participating in an emotions group.[81] We talked a lot about this quality in a previous chapter, given it's so deeply tied to the development of a Core Self. This is a double-edged trait. Awareness sheds light on every part of who we are, so when we are more committed to the protection of our Ideal Self than the emergence of our Core Self, it's easy to truncate any awareness that threatens those self-affirming ideals. Heart-Engaged leaders are confident enough to look into that mirror without flinching, trusting that the truth will indeed set them free.

Here's how Goleman defines self-aware people:

Aware of their moods as they are having them, these people understandably have some sophistication about their emotional lives. Their clarity about emotions may undergird other personality traits: they are autonomous and sure of their own boundaries, are in good psychological health, and tend to have a positive outlook on life. When they get into a bad mood, they don't ruminate and obsess about it, and are able to get out of it sooner. In short, their mindfulness helps manage their emotions.[82]

Sounds pretty good, doesn't it? Too good, in fact, not to fumble forward in this adventurous journey called emotionally intelligent living.

Look at how self-awareness helped Nathan and Jerry. Both discovered something remarkable in their marriages as they learned to check in with themselves. Two individuals, two different EQ groups, but the same illuminating revelation. Nathan and Jerry both came to their own realization that they were carrying a belief that they were better than their spouse. Smarter, wiser, and healthier. Somehow pride and arrogance crept into their construct of Self in ways they didn't notice. Until now.

It was humbling, and, of course, this revelation unlocked unprecedented opportunity for repair and realignment in their marriages. "My emotions allowed me the altitude to see that I have operated as if my life and story are good while hers are broken. I am the hero, and she is the victim," confessed Jerry. No more, though. This newfound awareness allowed intimacy to be rekindled for both of these leaders.

Taylor's experience was quite different. Her awareness of others has been sharpened to a keen edge, with little to none of this gift turned toward herself. Over the years, I listened with rapt attention as Taylor offered commentary and perspective on the situations of others. The complexity she can see and articulate is nothing short of amazing.

Such perception is riveting, yet when I attempt to direct the attention to her own situation, the resistance is instantaneous. She makes herself off-limits to everyone, including herself—the dysfunction is exacerbated by her overinvestment in others. She is one of the least self-aware people I know. She is simply unwilling or unable to transfer the same skillset into her own life, much to the detriment of her potential for growth and development.

The self-aware leader, in contrast, is someone who can see more than what meets the eye, in self as well as others. And the combination of this attribute together with emotional perspective begins to unlock the rare capacity of *wisdom*. It's easier to gain knowledge than wisdom, but both come to the fore as we become more self-aware and subsequently, more aware of others. This becomes the vantage point that activates keen sight for decision making, strategy building, and collaborative culture-crafting.

As the full scope of feelings is noticed and welcomed in step two, self-awareness gives birth to **Emotional Perspective**—a hugely valuable commodity for all of us. When we turn off the autopilot of habituated, unconscious, emotional reactions and learn to hold our feelings with curiosity and insight, our ability to perceive the emotional landscape opens up dramatically. Suddenly, a panorama of dimension and possibility appears, and we can respond to life situations with clear-sighted leadership. What a relief. We see more widely, and we see what's present more clearly. Who wouldn't want this as a resource?

Remember how workhorses used to have their vision constricted by blinders on each side? Blinders limited distraction and kept them focused on the task at hand. If you only have one job to do, it's brilliant. But leadership, by definition, requires a broad view so as to coordinate multiple people who are working on multiple projects simultaneously. Without emotional perspective, we're left with tunnel-vision, and that's bad news for leadership effectiveness.[83]

As we learn how to gain more emotional perspective, we can start to access more wisdom and discernment. We become more Creative, Accountable, Reflective, and (dare I say) Enlightened. Yes, enlightenment isn't just the domain of mountaintop gurus; it's the reward for every emotionally intelligent leader who has done the work we've laid out in this book.

I'd like to explore creativity with you for just a minute. Emotional creativity means allowing wonder into your life. Instead of reacting or avoiding when confronted with a dilemma, you let yourself wonder about it. Anchored in self-confidence, supported by self-control, resourced by self-awareness, you can follow your curiosity, knowing you have a whole palette of creative solutions at your disposal.

Creativity is the opposite of conclusiveness. Ever walk into a meeting or a relationship and know all is not well by the body language of others? My natural inclination here is to retreat, but I am learning to reach for emotional curiosity instead and to access the enlightenment that is always available to me. It's easy to assume that if others are agitated, we are the problem, but the creative, enlightened leader withholds judgment until the truth is unearthed.

Even if you are the problem, you can be curious about that and trust that here, too, a creative solution is available; and if the problem is elsewhere, you have everything you need to address that as well. Creative curiosity means asking when you don't know the answer, and this posture allows you to come alongside others and be fully present to them as the answer reveals itself.

Try this on for size: "I notice you seem agitated, and I wonder if it is because I am home thirty minutes late?" Or this one, "What's behind your sadness? I would love to be with you in it." These are undefended, open-hearted postures that allow us to enter someone else's emotional world in a safe way. Could these questions blow up? Of course; there are no magic wands for relational turmoil. But remember, we're learning to be leaders who face our lives rather than bury them.

Self-Worth

We can expect to find Self-Worth rising as we learn how to start paying attention to our feelings. The more we assign worth to our essential self, the more we will ascribe worth to others. And, of course, the opposite is also true: the lack of self-worth will lead you to devalue those around you. These dynamics are simply joined at the hip.

Self-worth also has an interesting relationship to self-confidence; they can either be partners in crime or the dream team because of the way they negatively or positively reinforce one another. As you begin to value your core essence, confidence emerges, along with the ability to express that value in the real world. When someone else validates your competencies and capabilities as a leader, this in turn trickles down to affirm your value. But when your confidence takes a hit, your self-worth will feel the aftershocks.

Heart-Engaged leaders are not trying to fight against these realities but rather, learning how to pay attention and make the connections. Matt tells me in an interview, "So much of my story has all been tied to *not being enough*. As a result, I have always pushed myself to excel and win, to try to prove that I have what it takes. The problem was that my self-worth was tethered to my achievements, so my personal value constantly rose and fell in the volatile stock market of life. That's an exhausting way to live. Now that I'm doing my work in the EQ System, I'm realizing that my worth is intrinsic; I am valuable for being me, which, interestingly enough, empowers my achievements more authentically than my old insecure self. Now I work because I *am* enough, not to *become* enough." That's a game-changer.

Self-worth is difficult to cultivate for many who learned from a young age that love is earned. Why do you love a newborn child? Infants don't do much more than eat, pee, poop, cry, smile, roll around, and look ridiculously cute. For quite a while, babies are takers, not contributors, yet we value that child's life as if it were our own. We offer babies gratuitous worth until they learn to offer it to themselves. Both babies and the elderly remind us that we are each worthy of love, care, and respect quite apart from what we accomplish.

Leaders learning to recognize and name their feelings constructively will begin to experience **Emotional Connection**. Yes, this dexterity of language and comfort with your emotional content helps you feel more deeply connected with yourself and others. This is golden for so many reasons.

Connection is intrinsically rewarding because the need for a tribe is hard-wired into our DNA. And when it comes to the workplace, leadership without connection is manipulation. It's that simple. And no one wants to be manipulated.

Emotional connection is a fascinating counterpart to emotional perspective. Different, yet complimentary. They push and pull together as do many of the core outcomes we're discussing. Connection reaches for the "trees," while perspective sees the "forest" and possibly even the mountains, streams, animals, and sky. How can we work to strengthen and cultivate both?

Heart-Engaged leaders are becoming more **Compassionate**, **Authentic**, **Relational**, and **Empathetic**. Can you feel the connective tissue within each of these characteristics and the potential they hold to deepen your personal and professional life?

Do you want your employees to have a healthy sense of loyalty and trust in you? The research says it's compassion that gets you there quicker than being a hard ass.[84] But if you have learned anything from this book, you'll remember that you can't offer something to others that you haven't given to yourself.

"Self-compassion is associated with less anxiety, depression, loneliness, and self-criticism and greater emotional coping skills, resilience, feelings of social connectedness, and healthier interpersonal relationships." This is from Ricks Warren in the department of psychiatry at the University of Michigan.[85] Compassion also has a direct correlation with what is arguably the greatest single characteristic of an emotionally intelligent leader: *Empathy.*

Empathy is the ability to understand, enter, and share another's emotional world in a way that is safe for both you and that person. Safe for you in that you can participate in people's feelings without losing your own equilibrium. Safe for the other person in that you enter that space without hijacking it for your own purposes.

I have a dear friend whose marriage is crumbling before his grieving eyes. This has not been my story, and I'm grateful for that, but I can empathetically connect to his story as he fluctuates between feelings of fear, anxiety, rage, powerlessness, and despair. These feelings are familiar enough for me to enter his world with solidarity. I can do nothing to fix his marriage or solve his problems, but I can offer him a communal space to feel the feelings of a desperate situation and know that he's not alone.

We could rightly say that empathy is the capacity and readiness to enter someone's emotional condition . . . with love, which brings us to our final, and perhaps most important topic of this book.

Above All Else, Love

The Beatles said, "All you need is love." Sarah McLachlan said that love is better than ice cream. And you know how good ice cream is. The Bible says that above all, we must love each other deeply because love covers a multitude of sins. Gandhi said, "Where there is love, there is life." And Tina Turner at least asked, "What's love got to do, got to do with it?"

I have a few tattoos. Okay, a lot of them. In my early twenties, I asked myself what life was about and came to realize that I needed guiding motivations more than specific destinations. On the inside of my left arm are the words, "Love God, Love Others." These words continue to guide my daily movements.

Something in my younger self was seeking to distill the complexities of this experience we call "life" into a simple and pervasive truth. Love became my guiding motivation. The decades have deepened and textured my understanding of love, but I am still 1,000 percent convinced that love is the one necessary foundation for life to be good and for all humans, teams, companies, and communities to thrive.

Much has been spoken and written and woven into every artful medium on this great topic, and I think many of these messages are true. Love makes the world go round. Without love, a thanksgiving meal, a marriage, a friendship, a team, or a company eventually grinds to a halt. Without love, we're left managing transactions, and those all come to an end sooner or later.

Not much, however, has been said about the role of love in leadership. I believe there are no great leaders without great love. And if love is the endgame for all human community, it must occupy a central place in our commerce. *Love will either be nurtured or eroded in the place we spend most of our waking hours.*

A seasoned executive leader lamented to me recently, "I have been on this planet for 70-plus years now, and there has been a decline in capacity for how people love and care for each other at home and work. There is little curiosity and attention left in this fast-paced world where conversation has been relegated to communication. People don't want to know me, ask questions, to care, or empathize. They only want to talk about themselves."

This is a sad commentary, but I think we see some truth in it. Can that trend be reversed? I think it can. Because we are limited and fallible, our intentions to love, like everything in this life, get twisted, diverted, and trumped by self-centeredness. But we get to write our story afresh each new day. We have the power to change the plotline.

As I grew older, I came to realize that my tattoo was missing something. I had started strong but overlooked a vital component: *Loving yourself.* The trifecta of health for me now is to, "Love God, Love Yourself, and Love Others."

If you're not spiritually minded, you can still engage the last two.

I am not talking about the narcissistic, egocentric, self-serving examples we see so much of in the news. I am talking about a healthy diet of self-love. It's really impossible to love others if you don't love yourself, which Jesus alluded to when he followed the greatest commandment of loving God with the second: to "love your neighbor as yourself."[86]

Loving yourself means living in the tension of your best and your worst, finding ways to reconcile the two, and still saying, *This is me.* I will keep showing up, and I will keep leaning in.

All this work in the EQ System secretly invites us into a life in which we are able to better love and care for ourselves and then have more to offer others in kind. Love makes great cultures, strong relationships, and healthy homes. We can't afford to neglect it in any venue.

"One of the persistent myths of the employer-employee or leader-follower relationship is 'Leaders should maintain an arms-length relationship with those with whom they work. In contrast with this commonly-held business assumption . . . are scholars who suggest that the leader-follower association is actually highly personal and that the wisest leaders will create relationships based upon a leader's genuine love for others."[87]

Do I love my employees? That can feel a little awkward to answer unless we bail out with the watered-down version of, "I love you, bro!" But yes, I do love my employees,

LOVING YOURSELF MEANS
LIVING IN THE TENSION OF
YOUR BEST AND YOUR WORST,
FINDING WAYS TO RECONCILE
THE TWO, AND STILL SAYING,
THIS IS ME. I WILL KEEP
SHOWING UP, AND I WILL
KEEP LEANING IN.

and I want to express my care for them in ways they can tangibly feel. My desire is to value them as *human beings* more than *human doings*. Love covers both the being and doing sides. Author Tommy Spaulding is more direct: "Leading from the heart means leading with love. If this word scares you, then use the word passion, commitment, compassion, servant-leadership, purpose-driven, mission-driven, or your choice of any similar word or phrase, because at the core these are all forms of love. In this context, love is simply an unselfish and genuine concern for the good of others."[88]

Business professor Raj Sisodia collected research to validate that businesses were more profitable when powered by a loving culture rather than a self-centered one. Some of us know that intuitively, but it's nice to see the data back it up because few businesses make love a priority at any level.

In his cleverly titled book *Firms of Endearment*, Sisodai goes to prove that loving companies develop a highly productive ethos and out-performed the S&P 500 by fourteen times and Good to Great Companies by six times over a period of fifteen years.[89] Impressive and inspiring. I mean, which company would you want to work for—one that captures your passion or merely your hours?

"Some very well-known companies such as Whole Foods (founder John Mackey dedicates a whole chapter to love in his book *Conscious Capitalism*) and Southwest Airlines (their NYSE ticker code is LUV) make explicit reference to love. In leadership writing, one of the most widely sold leadership textbooks (*The Leadership Challenge* by James Kouzes and Barry Posner) concludes that love is 'the secret to life' and consider it the 'best kept secret' of great leadership."[90] That's strong.

Vanderbilt University School of Medicine professor Wes Ely reflects, "As I've grown older, I have allowed myself to move from a purely cerebral approach at the bedside to a more emotional one. I've come to understand that my medical knowledge and technical skills are important in caring for my patients, but alone they are not good enough. Now I want to open myself up to what my patient is feeling and thinking, and to how I can best support his needs."[91]

Can we do the same for business as is happening in medicine? What would it take for us to include both the metrics of profit and production and the actual people behind the products? I'd like to find out. And we *are* finding out in our work at Transformed Leader, one cohort at a time, one company at a time. Both anecdotes and data are converging to form an inescapable message: Love wins.

We're all in process with this vision, and I hope I have inspired you to move much more intentionally in the direction of emotional intelligence for the sake of love. Yes, to fight for heart. I've offered you a system for taking practical steps—steps that are changing lives every day. I'll also offer a caution: Rather than preach this message right off the bat, just start living into it. Cultural norms aren't changed overnight—not internally, and not externally. Simply practice these principles and process them until they become part of your DNA. Once people start commenting on the changes they are experiencing in you, either at home or at work, then you can tell them why and invite them to join.

If we're honest, feelings often hurt like hell. And yet without our feelings, we would be lost—emotionally adrift in a meaningless world. So how can we build a courageous relationship with our emotional worlds in the hope that we can live with more connection, more significance, and more to offer those we serve?

Just as a healthy body requires an unrestricted blood flow in our veins, so our emotional hearts need clear, facilitated channels to carry their life through us and out to others. Heart-less or Heart-Engaged? The choice speaks for itself. It's time to take your emotional health as seriously as your physical health. And now you know how.

Personally, I want to connect my work with a grander purpose. I want my life to improve the experience of everyone I touch. I want to feel intimately connected to something bigger and more meaningful than myself. And if you've read this far, I think you want those things too.

So let's redefine what it means to win as a leader. You don't hear people on their deathbeds talking about the extra money they didn't make or projects they didn't complete. As we take our last breath on this planet, we want to know that we fought hard and lived deeply. We want to know that our lives mattered. That people will give a damn when we are gone because we meant so much to them. I don't always appreciate every feeling I have, but I am terribly grateful to be embracing more of my humanity than ever before. And I think that's at least part of the reason I do this work with others—to keep moving forward on this journey that matters so very much. I want to know myself and know others so that I can love better. Believe better. Live and lead better. Let's do this. Let's fight for what matters most.

Heart.

Endnotes

1. Chao Miao, Ronald H. Humphrey, and Shanshan Qian, "Emotional Intelligence and Authentic Leadership: A Meta Analysis," *Leadership & Organization Development Journal*, Iss. 0143-7739, June 11, 2018.

2. Robert Murray, *Exploring the Leadership Implications of Leaders Who Are Actively Practicing to Identify, Express, and Explore their Emotions in a Group*, PhD diss., (www.drrobmurray.com/research, 2022), 44-45.

3. Richard Weissbourd, Milena Batanova, Virginia Lovison, and Eric Torres, "Loneliness in America: How the Pandemic Has Deepened an Epidemic of Loneliness and What We Can Do About It" (Making Caring Common Project, 2021), https://mcc.gse.harvard.edu/reports/loneliness-in-america.

4. Jan Bergstrom, *Gifts from a Challenging Childhood: Creating A Practice for Becoming Your Healthiest Self* (Mountain Stream Publishing Company, 2019), 81.

5. Lindsay C. Gibson, *Adult Children of Emotionally Immature Parents: How to Heal from Distant, Rejecting, or Self-Involved Parents* (California, New Harbinger Publications, 2015), 145.

6. Daniel Goleman, *Emotional Intelligence: Why It Can Matter More than IQ, 10th Ed.* (New York, Bantam Books, 2005).

7. Marc Brackett PhD, *Permission to Feel: Unlocking the Power of Emotions to Help Our Kids, Ourselves, and Our Society Thrive* (New York, Celadon Books, 2020), 23.

8. Köppe, C., Held, M. J., & Schütz, A. (2019). "Improving Emotion Perception and Emotion Regulation Through a Web-based Emotional Intelligence Training (WEIT) Program for Future Leaders." (*International Journal of Emotional Education*, 2019), 11(2), 17-32.

9. Ernest Becker, *The Denial of Death* (New York, Free Press Paperbacks, a Division of Simon & Schuster, 1997).

10. Murray, 44, 45.

11. Mark Robert Waldman and Chris Manning PhD, *NeuroWisdom: The New Brain Science of Money, Happiness, and Success* (New York, Diversion Books, A Division of Diversion Publishing Corp., 2019). Epigraph.

12. Rebecca Hersher interview with Lisa Feldman Barrett, "The Making Of Emotions, From Pleasurable Fear To Bittersweet Relief," (NPR, June 1, 2017), https://www.npr.org/sections/health-shots/2017/06/01/530103479 /the-making-of-emotions-from-pleasurable-fear-to-bittersweet-relief.

13. Ibid.

14. Daniel J. Siegel, *Mindsight: The New Science of Personal Transformation* (New York, Bantam Books Trade Paperback, 2010).

15. "The Founding Fathers of Psychology," (Mibba), http://www.mibba.com /Articles/Science/6533/The-Founding-Fathers-of-Psychology/, Retrieved Nov. 21, 2022.

16. Peter Salovey and David J. Sluyter, *Emotional Development and Emotional Intelligence: Educational Implications* (Basic Books, 1997).

17. Brené Brown, "Developing Brave Leaders and Courageous Cultures," https://brenebrown.com/hubs/dare-to-lead/.

18. Marc Brackett PhD, *Permission to Feel: Unlocking the Power of Emotions to Help Our Kids, Ourselves, and Our Society Thrive* (New York, Celadon Books, 2020), 236.

19. Colleen Stanley, *Emotional Intelligence for Sales Success: Connect with Customers and Get Results* (New York, Atlanta, Brussels, Chicago, Mexico City, San Francisco, Shanghai, Tokyo, Toronto, Washington, D.C., AMACOM, American Management Association, 2012), 11.

20. Frederic Laloux, *Reinventing Organizations: A Guide to Creating Organizations Inspired by the Next Stage in Human Consciousness* (Nelson Parker, 2014), 143.

21. Daniel Goleman, *HBR's 10 Must Reads on Emotional Intelligence: What Makes a Leader?* (Boston, Harvard Business Review Press, 2015), 1.

22. Rob Murray, Jack Nicholson, and Jerome Daley, *The Human Operating System: Recovering the Heart and Soul of Your Leadership* (Telocity Media, 2021).

23. Murray, 47, 48.

24. Bill George, *Herminia Ibarra, Rob Goffee, Gareth Jones, Authentic Leadership, HBR Emotional Intelligence Series,* (Boston, Harvard Business Review Press, 2017) 14.

25. Murray, 53.

26. Lauren Landry, "Why Emotional Intelligence Is Important in Leadership," https://online.hbs.edu/blog/post/emotional-intelligence-in-leadership.

27. Ibid.

28. Daniel Goleman, *HBR's 10 Must Reads on Emotional Intelligence: What Makes a Leader?* (Boston, Harvard Business Review Press, 2015), 7.

29. Susan David, *Emotional Agility: Get Unstuck, Embrace Change, and Thrive in Work and Life* (New York, Avery, an imprint of Penguin Random House, 2016), 145.

30. Adapted from Richard Rohr, "*Unveiling the Shadow*," (Center for Action and Contemplation, June 13, 2021), https://cac.org/daily-meditations/unveiling-the-shadow-2021-06-13/.

31. John Naisbitt, *Megatrends: Ten New Directions Transforming Our Lives* (Warner Books, Inc., 1982).

32. Laloux, 37-38.

33. Ibid.

34. Travis Bradberry and Jean Greaves, *Emotional Intelligence 2.0* (Unabridged ed.), (Brilliance Audio, 2010), 13.

35. Murray, Nicholson, Daley, 86.

36. Lisa Feldman Barrett, *How Emotions Are Made: The Secret Life of the Brain* (Boston, New York, Houghton Mifflin Harcourt, 2017), 181.

37. Marc Brackett PhD, *Permission to Feel: Unlocking the Power of Emotions to Help Our Kids, Ourselves, and Our Society Thrive* (New York, Celadon Books), 49.

38. Ching-Sheue Fu, "What Are Emotions in Chinese Confucianism," (Research Gate, 2012), https://www.researchgate.net/publication/267228910_What_are_emotions_in_Chinese_Confucianism.

39. Chip Dodd, *The Voice of the Heart: A Call to Full Living*, 2nd Ed. (Nashville, Sage Hill Resources, 2014), 100.

40. Ibid., 104.

41. Lisa Feldman Barrett, *How Emotions Are Made the Secret Life of the Brain* (Boston, New York, Houghton Mifflin Harcourt, 2017).

42. Kendra Cherry, "*The Yerkes-Dodson Law and Performance*" (*Very Well Mind*, May 24, 2022).

43. "Control anger before it controls you," (American Psychological Association, March 3, 2022), https://www.apa.org/topics/anger/control.

44. "Anger," (*Psychology Today*), https://www.psychologytoday.com/us/basics/anger.

45. Definition of "Sensationalism," *Google Dictionary Box, Oxford Lexicon.*

46. June Price Tangney and Kurt W. Fischer, *Self-Conscious Emotions: The Psychology of Shame, Guilt, Embarrassment, and Pride* (New York, The Guilford Press, 1995), 24.

47. Preeti Aroon, "*China Bans Unauthorized Reincarnations*," (*Foreign Policy*, August 29, 2007), https://foreignpolicy.com/2007/08/29/china-bans-unauthorized-reincarnations/.

48. Helen Block Lewis, *Shame and Guilt in Neurosis* (International Universities Press, 1971), 30.

49. Brené Brown, *Daring Greatly: How the Courage to Be Vulnerable Transforms the Way We Live, Love, Parent, and Lead* (New York, Avery, an imprint of Penguin Random House, 2012), 67.

50. June Price Tangney and Kurt W. Fischer, *Self-Conscious Emotions: The Psychology of Shame, Guilt, Embarrassment, and Pride* (New York, London, The Guilford Press, 1995), 295.

51. Dodd, 49.

52. Dodd, 44.

53. "Transforming Pain," (Center for Action and Contemplation, October 17, 2018), Adapted from Richard Rohr, *A Spring Within Us: A Book of Daily Meditations*, (CAC Publishing: 2016), 199, 120-121.

54. Alyssa Fowers and William Wan, "*A third of Americans now show signs of clinical anxiety or depression, Census Bureau finds amid coronavirus pandemic*," (*Washington Post*, May 26, 2020), https://www.washingtonpost .com/health/2020/05/26/americans-with-depression-anxiety-pandemic/.

55. Elisabeth Kübler-Ross and David Kessler, *On Grief and Grieving: Finding the Meaning of Grief Through the Five Stages of Loss* (New York, London, Toronto, Sydney, Scribner, 2005).

56. "Loneliness in the Workplace: 2020 U.S. Report," (Cigna, January 2020), https://www.cigna.com/static/www-cigna-com/docs/about-us/newsroom /studies-and-reports/combatting-loneliness/cigna-2020-loneliness-report.pdf.

57. Ibid.

58. Elena Renken, "Most Americans Are Lonely And Our Workplace Culture May Not Be Helping," (NPR, January 2020), https://www.cigna.com/static /www-cigna-com/docs/about-us/newsroom/studies-and-reports/combatting -loneliness/cigna-2020-loneliness-report.pdf.

59. Richard Schwartz PhD, *No Bad Parts: Healing Trauma and Restoring Wholeness with the Internal Family Systems Model* (Boulder, Colorado, Sounds True, 2021), 4.

60. Ibid., 17.

61. Alessandro Grecucci1, Irene Messina, Letizia Amodeo, Gaia Lapomarda, Cristiano Crescentini, Harold Dadomo, Marta Panzeri, Anthony Theuninck and Jon Frederickson, "A Dual Route Model for Regulating Emotions: Comparing Models, Techniques, and Biological Mechanisms," (Frontiers, June 4, 2020), https://www.frontiersin.org/articles/10.3389/fpsyg.2020.00930/full.

62. Ingrid Bacon, Elizabeth McKay, Frances Reynolds, and Anne McIntyre, "The Lived Experience of Codependency: an Interpretive Phenomenological Analysis," (Springer Link, August 21, 2018), https://link.springer.com/article /10.1007/s11469-018-9983-8.

63. Dan McAdams, "Human motives and personal relationships," *Communication, intimacy, and close relationships*, (New York, Academic Press) 41-70.

64. R. A. Masters, *Emotional Intimacy: A Comprehensive Guide for Connecting with the Power of Your Emotions* (Boulder, Colorado, Sounds True, 2013), 2.

65. Chao Miao, Ronald H. Humphrey, and Shanshan Qian, "Emotional intelligence and authentic leadership: a meta-analysis" (*Leadership & Organization Development Journal*, Iss. 0143-7739, June 11, 2018).

66. Murray, 59.

67. Peter F. Drucker, *The Five Most Important Questions You Will Ever Ask About Your Organization* (Jossey-Bass, A Wiley Imprint, 2008), 53, 59.

68. Dan Ariely, "You Are What You Measure," (*Harvard Business Review*, June 2010), https://hbr.org/2010/06/column-you-are-what-you-measure.

69. Ibid.

70. Murray, Nicholson, Daley, 27.

71. Emotional intelligence can be trained and developed, which suggests that organizations could benefit from having their leaders participate in emotional intelligence development training (Köppe et al., 2019; Mattingly & Kraiger, 2019).

72. Murray, 54.

73. Daniel Goleman, *Working with Emotional Intelligence* (New York, Toronto, London, Sydney, Auckland, Bantam Books, 2000), 86.

74. Murray, 54.

75. Marie Norman and Terry Hyland, "The Role of Confidence in Lifelong Learning," (Research Gate, June 2003), https://www.researchgate.net/publication/233661460_The_Role_of_Confidence_in_Lifelong_Learning.

76. Susan David, *Emotional Agility: Get Unstuck, Embrace Change, and Thrive in Work and Life* (New York, Avery, an imprint of Penguin Random House, 2016), 5.

77. Diane Coutu, "How Resilience Works," (*Harvard Business Review*, 2002), 10.

78. Mysirlaki, S., & Paraskeva, F. (2020), "Emotional intelligence and transformational leadership in virtual teams: lessons from MMOGs," (*Leadership & Organization Development Journal, V. 41, no.4, 551-566, May 2020*), https://doi.org/10.1108/LODJ-01-2019-0035.

79. "Self Control," (*Psychology Today*), https://www.psychologytoday.com/us/basics/self-control.

80. M. Muraven, R. Baumeister, "Self-Regulation and Depletion of Limited Resources: Does Self-Control Resemble a Muscle?," v. 126, no. 2 (*Psychological Bulletin*, 2000), 248.

81. Murray, 54.

82. Daniel Goleman, *Emotional Intelligence: Why It Can Matter More Than IQ, 10th Ed* (Bantam, 2005), 48.

83. Madhulika Sarkar and Shelly Oberoi, "Emotional Intelligence: An Extensive Literature Review," v. 10, no. 3, (*Global Journal of Enterprise Information System*), 84-94.

84. Daniel Goleman, Annie McKee, and Adam Waltz, *Empathy: HBR Emotional Intelligence Series*, (Harvard Review Business Press, 2017), 16.

85. Ricks Warren, "Emotion regulation in borderline personality disorder: The role of self-criticism, shame, and self-compassion," (Wiley Periodicals, Inc., January 21, 2015), https://deepblue.lib.umich.edu/handle/2027.42/110727.

86. Matthew 22:39.

87. Verl Anderson, Cam Caldwell, and Blair Barfuss, "Love: The Heart of Leadership," v. 22, iss. 2 (Graziadio Business Review, 2019).

88. Tommy Spaulding, *The Heart-Led Leader: How Living and Leading from the Heart Will Change Your Organization and Your Life* (New York, Currency, 2015), 2.

89. Rajendra Sisodia, David Wolfe, Jagdish Sheth, *Firms of Endearment* (New Jersey, Pearson Education, 2014).

90. Duncan Coombe, "Can You Really Power an Organization with Love?" (*Harvard Business Review*, 2016).

91. Wes Ely, *Every Deep-Drawn Breath: A Critical Care Doctor on Healing, Recovery, and Transforming Medicine in the ICU* (New York, London, Toronto, Sydney, New Delhi, Scribner, 2021), 181.

Index

A

"A, B, C's" of becoming Heart-Engaged, 234, 235
acceptance, 173–174
action, 126–127, 232–233
adaptation, feelings and, 22–26
Adler, Alfred, 56, 57–58
advocacy, 138, 140
aggression, 202
agility, emotional, 93–95, 239
Ariely, Dan, 232
American Express, 61
anger, 134–135, 136–141, 162, 173, 184, 185
anterior cingulate, 53
anxiety, 121–122
apathy, 138, 175–176
archetypes
    The Caretaker, 200, 212–217
    The General, 200–206
    The Mythic, 200, 218–222
    overview of, 199
    The Trailblazer, 200, 206–212
arrogance, 125–126
avoidance, 175–176

B

bargaining, 173
Barrett, Karen Caplovitz, 146
Barrett, Lisa Feldman, 54, 113, 123

barriers, pushing through, 50–52
Bayer Laboratories, 51
The Beatles, 251
Becker, Ernest, 37
belonging, 160
blame, 147
Blind Self, 89
body, connecting to, 78
The Body Keeps the Score (van der Kolk), 78
Brackett, Marc, 31, 60, 113–114
brain, 52–55, 69–70
Brian, Montana, 211
Brown, Brené, 9, 59–60, 150, 170
Brunello di Montalcino 2012 wine, 230

C

calmness, 174–178, 184
care/cared for, 156–161, 184, 186
carelessness, 125–126
The Caretaker archetype, 200, 212–217
caretaking for others, 213
caretaking for self, 212–213
Carroll, Lewis, 76
catching up to yourself step, 76–81, 235
clarity, 176
codependency, 158–159, 216
collective unconscious, 56–57

CONNECT WITH ROB

CONSULTING

Transformed Leader is an action-research leadership firm that coaches and consults leaders, teams, and organizations into breakthrough levels of growth using the Human Operating Systems™ (HOS) leadership model. Heart, Soul, Mind, and Strength™ are the vital components of healthy leaders. **www.transformedleader.com**

SPEAKING

Rob Murray speaks to companies, associations, and leaders nationwide, challenging and inspiring audiences to navigate deep change and transformation. Invite him to share at your next event. **www.drrobmurray.com**

PODCAST

The Talk of Change podcast is a show designed to inspire and deepen your life and leadership at home and work. Rob Murray sits down with carefully selected leaders, experts, and guides to help listeners grow more capacity, connection, character, and courage. **www.talkofchange.com**

FACEBOOK, INSTAGRAM & MOST PLATFORMS
@drrobmurray

HEART-ENGAGED EQ™

CARDS TO DEEPEN YOUR LIFE, LOVE, AND LEADERSHIP

This card set and its companion book, *Fighting for Heart*, offer practical tools to recover your heart and grow your EQ in ways that can transform every aspect of your life and leadership. The Heart-Engaged EQ System is an experiential roadmap for individuals, teams, organizations, families, friends, educators, and counselors. It's like moving from monochrome to color. Life simply becomes more alive, opening doors to the things that matter most.

5 CHECK-INS

Core Self

Core Feelings

Core Characters

Core Outcomes

Picture Cards

Start building a courageous relationship
with your emotional world.
www.heartengaged.com

SHARE AND SUPPORT

Would you consider helping me share this book and work with others? I would deeply cherish your support in whatever ways you choose. One easy way would be to snap a photo of your favorite quotations on the following pages and post them to your social media accounts to inspire or challenge your family and friends to dive in.

Make sure to tag me at **@drrobmurray**.

Thank you in advance. Let's do this!

CONNECTION & COMMUNITY

You are only lonely
with people you want
more with.

———

#FIGHTINGFORHEART
@DRROBMURRAY

ACCEPTANCE & FAILURE

All humnas are fallible
and limited. If you learn
to accept this humble
reality, failure becomes
an avenue, not an
obstacle, to growth.

———

#FIGHTINGFORHEART
@DRROBMURRAY

Boxed wine gets the job done, but there is something mystical about a bottle that has been carefully considered, chosen, and laid down for a specific number of years to bring it to perfect maturity.

—

#FIGHTINGFORHEART
@DRROBMURRAY

Loving yourself means living in the tension of your best and your worst, finding ways to reconcile the two, and still saying, This is me. I will keep showing up, and I will keep leaning in.

—

#FIGHTINGFORHEART
@DRROBMURRAY

SOCIAL SHARES

HURT & HEALING

Saying you feel hurt is
deeply vulnerable and
brave despite what your
parents may have told
you growing up.

———

#FIGHTINGFORHEART
@DRROBMURRAY

SHAME & AVOIDANCE

When we can no longer metabolize
the feeling of shame, it's easy to try
to numb its debilitating voice with
over-indulgence and
self-medication. These escape
strategies are short-lived at best,
And at worst, can dismantle all that
is most precious to us.

———

#FIGHTINGFORHEART
@DRROBMURRAY

SOCIAL SHARES

ANGER & ANVOCACY

The feeling of healthy
anger reminds us that
something is wrong
and must be fixed or at
least considered.

———

#FIGHTINGFORHEART
@DRROBMURRAY

ANGER & CURIOSITY

Ask the next time you are
angry, "What else am I
feeling?" Sometimes anger
is a diversion from what's
really going on inside.

———

#FIGHTINGFORHEART
@DRROBMURRAY

New ideas and opportunities must first be unknown before they can be known, meaning we must enter unfamiliar territory to find new treasures.

———

#FIGHTINGFORHEART
@DRROBMURRAY

Confident leaders are those who can name their incompetence without fear or shame. Rather than being threatened or driven to pretense, they boldly acknowledge their limits and catalyze the gifts of others to address challenges and brings home the win.

———

#FIGHTINGFORHEART
@DRROBMURRAY

Feelings rarely need fixing; instead, they need to be identified, shared, and heard. Preferably by a compassionate witness rather than a strategic informant.

———

#FIGHTINGFORHEART
@DRROBMURRAY

Not all fear is bad. Being afraid to some degree helps us prepare and deliver. Fear drives action, and often that action requires courage. Using fear strategically helps us avoid panic responses and choose smart ones instead.

———

#FIGHTINGFORHEART
@DRROBMURRAY

SOCIAL SHARES

Feelings, like the color of our blood, like death and desire, remind us that we are all equally human, created with common realities, motivations, and bonds that transcend the intricacies of our individual lives.

———

#FIGHTINGFORHEART
@DRROBMURRAY

What are you feeling? Do you have people or places where you don't have to explain, defend, or justify your answers?

———

#FIGHTINGFORHEART
@DRROBMURRAY

SOCIAL SHARES

THE HUMAN OPERATING SYSTEM
Recovering the Heart and Soul of Your Leadership

Jack Nicholson and Dr. Rob Murray have been developing the Human Operating System™ (HOS) over many years of work with executive leaders, teams, and organizations. The deep change processes and principles embedded in the HOS have made a significant difference with leaders who have become frustrated, depleted, and fragmented, trying to build enterprises with tools and resources no longer sufficient.

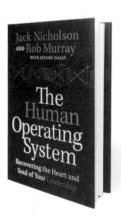

The Human Operating System™ is like the Amazon; it flows through the heart of leadership development like a mighty river. Applying the five transformative principles and processes in the HOS is so much more effective than hacking through the forest of leadership trade books, workshops, and management techniques. Many of these tools can be helpful, but they often function more like "Apps" or accessories rather than a deeper Operating System that can offer meaning, direction, and coherence to everything you might do as a Leader.

www.transformedleader.com